No Dancing, No Dancing:
Inside the Global Humanitarian Crisis

Denis Dragovic

No Dancing, No Dancing: Inside the Global Humanitarian Crisis
Published by Odyssey Books in 2018

Copyright © Denis Dragovic 2018
All rights reserved. No part of this book may be reproduced or transmitted by any person or entity, including internet search engines or retailers, in any form or by any means, electronic or mechanical, including photocopying (except under the statutory exceptions provisions of the Australian Copyright Act 1968), recording, scanning or by any information storage and retrieval system without the prior written permission of the publisher. www.odysseybooks.com.au

A Cataloguing-in-Publication entry is available from the National Library of Australia

ISBN: 978-1-925652-31-4 (pbk)
ISBN: 978-1-925652-32-1 (ebook)

Cover design by Owen Gibbons
Cover photo by Peter Biro

To my wife, who held her peace as I proposed the idea, and to my daughter, for whom I would think trice before taking such risks again.

And to my parents who bore the burden of worrying for my safety every minute of every day for year after year, thank you.

Contents

Preface	1
Part one: South Sudan	9
Rough neighbourhoods	11
Revolutionary bureaucrats	13
Spaghetti logic	40
The beauty returns	57
What it means to be human	65
A faltering façade	70
Part two: Iraq	77
A beard for every situation	79
Plotting an assassination	91
Divine intervention	102
Tales from an Ayatollah	111
Cause and effect	122
Political campaigning Iraqi style	135
Gifts for the governor	142
Ghost soldiers	147
Part three: East Timor	153
Kumbaya	155
The IQ of a Dog	158
Four languages, one country	161
Dangerous times	167
US Marines	173
Fish Farming in the Mountains	178
Part four: Reflections	187
About the Author	201

Preface

I once bought the life of a Sudanese man with eight cows. He'd accidentally killed a friend and had been sentenced to death, so I paid the remaining blood money just weeks before he was to hang. When we first met, I was a young humanitarian aid worker living in Wau, a battered Sudanese town under siege for most of the eighteen years of civil war in that country. A judge I had met through my work had invited me to visit the town's prisons to witness their judicial system, so I went—mostly out of curiosity.

From the outside, the jail's crumbling façade reflected the ravages of a country at war. I stood in the courtyard among the crowd of prisoners for a moment and looked around. Children were incarcerated alongside adults, housed in barracks without bunks or beds, only the cement floor to sleep on and each other's bodies to keep warm. Roofs had collapsed, whether neglect or war was to blame, I wasn't sure. I had free rein to walk around, though I didn't stray far. The prisoners seemed inactive and submissive, yet on edge, as if each was fighting his own battle for sanity. Freedom would have been an abstract thought, as discharge from the penitentiary would only release them into a city under siege. If they managed to escape from Wau they would still be prisoners, living free within the police state of the renegade Khartoum government.

Walking onto death row, I saw six latrine-sized cells smelling of faeces crowded around a lone tree. In its shade a rusted shackle was bolted to a cement block—furlough for prisoners or a restraining tool for the executioner? I didn't ask. The judge described each of the condemned men and their crimes, one after another, as they stood in the shadows of their cells looking back at us in silence. Then we came to Marco Garang. He was chained to the floor and dressed in ragged shards that would have once resembled clothes. The judge took his time in explaining the case while Marco's round face, missing his front two teeth and bereft of emotion, stared out at us, seemingly lost in his own world. The judge explained that Marco had come forward to the police, admitting to murdering his friend but blaming alcohol and a friendly tussle gone wrong for the terrible outcome. The judge I was with explained that, regrettably, tribal law didn't acknowledge accidental killing. An eye for an eye prevailed in this part of the world. He had killed his friend unintentionally, but under the law he had to die for it.

A few days later I met with Sister Sarah at the Comboni compound to speak about Marco. She was a quietly spoken Italian woman with twenty years of missionary work in Sudan under her belt. She knew him well, she told me, having prayed for forgiveness and a second chance for the young man whom she believed genuinely regretted his crime. She also explained that if the sentence was carried out, his family would be compelled to seek revenge against his accusers, perpetuating a cycle of blood feuds and killing. So I paid the remaining blood money, eight cows or about three hundred dollars, settling the debt due to the family of the dead man. It seemed the right thing to do, a small act of mercy in an otherwise merciless country at war with itself.

Yet for others more deserving of compassion, such as the dozen or so slaves, young boys and women rounded up from nearby villages not far from where I paid for Marco's life, I could only stand by and watch as their single-file shackled procession passed by. While Marco's nightmare ended with a simple transaction, theirs was only beginning when money changed hands between the slavers and those who decided to buy the lives of other humans. Somewhat bafflingly, the judge whose humanity had brought me to Marco asserted the righteousness of the slavers. He saw them not as traffickers in human misery but benefactors who would house, educate, and provide for children otherwise left with little to live for. To him, the chains and exchange of money were simply a part of what was the first step towards a better life.

In Iraq, the first female staff member I hired, a mother of two, was shot at her home, a senseless honour killing perpetrated by her brothers-in-law in response to rumours of infidelity. We broke internal policy by hiring her husband so that the children could continue to go to school. I didn't know those responsible, but we had heard of similar cases where brothers or fathers, perpetrators of the killings, spoke of their love for the slain woman.

Not long after, in late 2004, I was invited to step away for a moment from the improvised explosive devices and death threats in an ever-deteriorating Iraq and to slip into a tuxedo and black tie for the annual Freedom Awards dinner. The International Rescue Committee (IRC), a charity delivering humanitarian aid around the world, had been organising the award since 1957, and as the Country Director for Iraq I was invited to attend along with a few others who were posted in the field. It was a luxurious event held in the cavernous Grand Ballroom of the Waldorf Astoria Hotel in New York. The IRC has a team of staff working year-round to organise the event, and it showed as guests were seated, chandeliers dimmed, and the multimedia presentation began. Heart-wrenching pictures of starving children and displaced families slowly segued into scenes of IRC staff providing aid to the needy. It tugged at the heartstrings.

Diners parted with US $1,000 to enjoy an ordinary meal but extraordinary company. I sat a few tables from where Kofi Annan, then UN Secretary General, took centre stage. The Freedom Award was not given that year; instead, a Distinguished Humanitarian Award was presented to Lieutenant-General Romeo Dallaire, the former Head of Peacekeeping Operations in Rwanda. In 1994 he had become a symbol of the world's conscience after he asked for and was refused the right to intervene to stop the genocide. Instead, he watched along with millions of others throughout the world as the killing unfolded. Many subsequently asked: how could the West stand by and watch first hundreds, then thousands and then hundreds of thousands of people being slaughtered? As General Dallaire pleaded for support, the international community evaded calling the rolling massacre a genocide for fear of being compelled to act. As the days rolled into weeks, there were no street protests in Western capitals, no high-level resignations or damaging exposés of cover-ups. But on the streets of Africa, the West's inaction became a stain that left many questioning our humanity.

Recalling these memories—of Marco, the slave traders, the Iraqi honour killings and General Dallaire—is more than what is commonly referred to as poverty porn. Their stories leave questions. Is honour killing or slavery justified within the cultural norms of another society? If it isn't, then what is the right balance between a well-intentioned effort to change traditions and cultural imperialism? And even if we find that Goldilocks sweet spot and act appropriately to stop slavery, honour killings or genocide, but leave the job incomplete, have we done more harm than good? Maybe it took the lifeless body of Aylan Kurdi or the young Yazidi girls forced into slavery to take these issues from being dilemmas faced by a few into signs of an emerging global humanitarian crisis.

* * *

My parents moved to Australia in 1968, leaving behind not only their family but a future shaped by the politics of ethnicity. The civil war that spread through the former Yugoslavia in the nineties managed to overcome the tyranny of distance that protects Australians from such other-world events and changed our lives in the process, from our family and friends to the church we attended.

During those years, I would hear stories of threats to lives, houses burned, property stolen, and of escape. Sometimes the escape was psychological, compartmentalising life into neat boxes that separate the war from daily life as if the two could co-exist—by day fighting on the front lines, by night reading bedtime stories to children. For others, it was an escape into isolation that bred a raging anger, or a fear that couldn't be shaken, or worse still a deep melancholy that drained the will to live. Then there were those who escaped, fleeing their community or country. My maternal grandparents were forced to flee their homes becoming, in the industry lingo, IDPs, or internally displaced persons, while my paternal grandparents became refugees. I knew the facts of the war, read the news reports, heard the stories, but understood very little about its reality on the ground.

Two decades later, images of over a million people pushing through the borders of Europe, many through the familiar landscapes of Croatia and Serbia, reminded me of the Balkans wars. This time a decade of working in conflict zones provided a new perspective on war.

Widely reported as refugees fleeing Syria, the mass of humanity included people from countries as diverse as Pakistan, Nigeria, Ethiopia, and even the neighbouring Balkans. The human tsunami hit Europe four years after the Syrian conflict began, years after camps in the Middle East were filled to the brim, and more than a year after the rise of the fanatical Islamic State of Iraq and the Levant (ISIL/ISIS). This was the humanitarian crisis that gripped the world and divided European leaders. While much was said on what should be done, few asked the more important question. Not what had driven the people to flee, but why then and not earlier? What drove the people out of Syria was the civil war, a simple answer that offers an easy solution, an opportunity for politicians to act decisively by deploying military force. Discussing why at that point in time and not earlier is a much more complex but critical conversation.

For the European migration crisis, as with other humanitarian crises around the world, the background begins with local dynamics and power politics that are in turn shaped by tradition, religion, and culture. The West becomes involved through its diplomatic and military forays that together with an aid response shape the humanitarian situation on the ground, either successfully averting a crisis or adding fuel to the fire. In this case, the tinder was quickly drying as millions of people found themselves in a limbo living in camps and urban settlements throughout Turkey, Lebanon, and Jordan. They were living in temporary accommodation, drinking from temporary wells, working temporary jobs, and sending their children to temporary schools. The ground for a crisis had been laid through our reputation of being unable to see through a crisis, a condition known as donor fatigue.

What had begun as a fight of freedom against Bashar al-Assad became an existential conflict for many Syrians. Four million had fled across borders into camps and the community where Western donors provided support. Another eight million became internally displaced within Syria. For the first few years billions of dollars were channelled to humanitarian assistance supporting the refugees fleeing Syria, but donor fatigue set in and international attention shifted. In 2015, the year when the European migration crisis began, the United Nations' humanitarian appeal for Syria was only 35% funded. Which meant that food distribution in camps had to be cut in half, cash distribution to those living in the community dropped from $28 per month to $14, schools struggled to find funding, and health clinics had to be closed. Parents saw the writing on the wall. Stay in the camps and face a bleak future or with the meagre savings that remained buy passage to Europe. This was the dry tinder that was waiting for a spark to set alight the migration crisis.

I had experienced this before. Just as quickly as the international community's attention had focused upon Iraq in the years following the 2003 invasion, it shifted gears to George Clooney's Darfur and then the Indian Ocean tsunami, with each drawing press coverage and humanitarian dollars away from the one before.

Yet, for the people left behind their catastrophe continued. Their future could not remain on hold. Their lives were not temporary. I often wonder what happened to these people.

Understanding a conflict and the accompanying humanitarian crisis requires taking a step back from the regular press reporting on political machinations and the speeches of statesmen that see events as if they are planned and then coordinated by a deliberate hand. Scratch a little deeper and we see that often they are instead consequences of a spur of the moment decision driven by an individual's hopes, fears, or even simply ignorance. A single act creates a myth whose message spreads like wildfire, rippling through society and gaining momentum before turning into a movement—the anger of the street vendor in Tunisia that raised a revolution, or the courage of the first Syrian family to take the boat across the Aegean—setting the course for a million others to follow.

To understand the humanitarian consequences of war and better prepare a response, we need to engage with the stories of people before they become the news, we need to work outside the neat boxes that academia creates and instead embrace the interconnectedness that is the chaos of war. This book attempts to do that by following a journey I took travelling back to the places where I had worked between 2000 and 2010 as a humanitarian aid worker—Sudan, Iraq and East Timor. People are at the centre of this book, including those who depended upon the aid to survive, community leaders who advised on its disbursement, or the local aid workers lending their insights and skills to the endeavour. They are also the ones who tell the story of what worked and what didn't. By returning to these countries to see what happened to the aid projects, this book sheds light on how we can better respond to the emerging global humanitarian crisis.

PART ONE
South Sudan

Rough neighbourhoods

There are a handful of places that manage to consistently appear at the bottom of country development lists, those that face the trifecta of war, disease and isolation. Many of these are in Sub-Saharan Africa. A rough historical guide to some of these countries' past would read: slavers raid villages, plundering and pillaging. Colonisation stops the slavery but continues the plunder. White man's burden grows too heavy as nationalistic sentiment develops. Independence struggle leads to nationhood, but with some very heavy strings attached. Charismatic freedom fighter turns into demagogic messiah-complex strongman who takes charge as the dreams of a new dawn fade. Resources continue to be pillaged, millions appropriated. War inevitably returns.

If the people are lucky the war will be a coup that comes and goes, fought mainly by soldiers and loyalists, rarely touching upon the lives of the civilians. But sometimes a nation's limited resources or its people's will are not enough to match a leader's ambitions. At the pronouncement of a politician's speech (Milosevic in the Balkans) or a disk jockey's vitriol (Radio Rwanda), previously contained undercurrents of resentment and disenfranchisement are co-opted into a fabricated historic struggle that reaches deep into the people's psyche and stokes the embers of ancient hatred.

These wars are the most devastating as they destroy the social fabric of a society. The wealthiest flee at the outbreak, saving themselves and their relatives, transferring cash, selling assets, and moving to neighbouring countries or the West. As the war continues and shows no respite, the middle class follow in their footsteps, selling what little they have remaining, moving to neighbouring countries, paying people smugglers or waiting out the long bureaucratic process of asylum applications. The poorest tend to leave last, if at all, as they have fewer resources with which to start anew, so they remain behind, buffeted by the winds of war.

Infrastructure and valuable assets including machinery and industrial equipment, essential to any economic recovery, are stripped bare by the owners as the conflict nears, during the war by soldiers and profiteers, or immediately after by the newly anointed 'legitimate owners'.

The young, having missed years of education, are shell-shocked and traumatised, a generation or two or even three, lost. In some cases, where the war rages for years, even cleared farmland disappears as nature follows in the soldiers' footsteps, obliterating the last remaining signs of civilisation.

South Sudan is one such place.

Revolutionary bureaucrats

I looked down at the lush landscape of northern Kenya as I flew from Nairobi to what was then the capital of the autonomous region of South Sudan, Juba. My hope was to spend as much face-to-face time with the local people, engaging with them and seeing how their daily lives had changed since the last time I had been there. Cars and buses were in and planes and helicopters were out. That's how I found myself stranded on a dirt road surrounded by high grass, scattered trees and a few low-lying hills as far as the eye could see. Mundri, the location of a former aid program that I was involved in, was still another hundred and sixty kilometres away.

As soon as I had landed in Juba, James Amule, a former colleague during my time with CHF International, a US-based humanitarian organisation (since renamed Global Communities), had arranged a vehicle for my journey into the hinterland. I told him that I didn't have a lot of money to spend so he found a car that met my budget. It had already broken down once earlier in the day. At that stop Abdi, my hired driver, had caught a ride back into town to buy a new fan belt, but he didn't take the old one with him so two hours later he returned with a wrong-sized replacement. After another two-hour wait for a second trip into town we were on our way again, only to break down once more.

Abdi assured me in Arabic that it wasn't a problem, though I couldn't get more out of him as my Arabic was limited and his English virtually non-existent. I wondered what possessed James to find the one driver in Juba who wasn't from the south and couldn't even speak English. Abdi stood out amongst the crowd of tall and muscular men of the various southern Sudanese tribes. I later learned that he was from Darfur, which explained his shorter frame and slightly lighter skin as well as his Arabic.

Questions started to circle in my mind as I watched him tinker under the hood, including why Abdi didn't carry a toolkit in the car. We had to flag down a passing bus to borrow a set of pliers. Why was there a spare fuel pump in the back seat that didn't fit the car? This seemed a particularly relevant question as the current problem appeared to be the fuel pump. I also started to think about what I was going to do if we were stuck for the night. There was no town within walking distance and most of the traffic passing through was the UN and NGO type that sped by at top speed with little or no concern for the broken down car by the side of the road.

Earlier in the day, during the intervals when the car was functioning and we were moving, I peppered Abdi with as many questions as my limited Arabic would allow. I was particularly interested in understanding how he had ended up in South Sudan since clearly he was not a southerner.

'Enta men when?' Where are you from? I asked, to which he gushed forth a long response that I had no chance of understanding.

So I'd repeat the same question until he'd respond in a way that used the handful of Arabic words I could understand. With each mile that we covered I got an additional snippet of information. He had fled Darfur when the fighting reached his village. Hoping to find a better and safer life in the south after the peace agreement was signed, he moved to Juba. He didn't speak English, but that didn't seem to deter him. Nor did he speak French, yet he was planning to cross the border into Chad and then to seek asylum in France. Based on my first day's impression I doubted whether he could organise himself to even make it to the border.

After cajoling some kids from a local village to help push start the car (the battery was dead by this time), but still to no avail, our options were running out. I was reluctantly considering jumping on the next bus back to Juba to start all over again when a convoy of Sudan People's Liberation Army soldiers passed by. Two Land Cruiser pickups filled to the brim with soldiers, over two dozen camouflage-clad, weapon-totting, mean-looking soldiers pulled up alongside us. To my surprise the driver jumped out to offer help. Taking the opportunity to stretch their legs, the entire contingent disembarked and suddenly we were surrounded by a platoon of soldiers offering opinions on what the problem was. The consensus was the fuel pump, but since it couldn't be fixed there was little that could be done. As the order was given to mount up, the general at the centre of the convoy asked me where I was headed.

'Mundri,' I replied.

'You can join us if you like,' he said, pointing to the back of the second car. I jumped at the opportunity to get moving but also to enjoy a change of company. Abdi assured me that he'd get the car to Mundri by the end of the day. I wasn't so sure, but going with the sentiment I left him some money to cover the costs and told him that I'd see him there. I grabbed my pack, threw it into the pickup and jumped on, joining the soldiers, their weapons, and gear.

There wasn't much of a conversation. None of the soldiers had gone to school so their English was limited and no one spoke any Arabic. The only information I managed to piece together was that I had jumped onto a convoy escorting General Kilo on a tour inspecting the garrisons throughout the south. I suspect that he had been tasked with evaluating military preparedness in the few short months leading up to the vote on independence.

Without much to discuss I focused on the scenery in front of me, distracted only by the machine gun muzzle that was uncomfortably nudging my back. The view was a blur of lush savannah, high grass, low lying shrubbery, and a mix of unfamiliar African trees. It wasn't the deepest, darkest Africa that most people associate with the continent; instead it was what looked to me like prime, but long untended and overgrown farming land.

There is a lot of talk, mostly in jest, that South Sudan could become the world's largest organic farm. The soil remains as it has been since time immemorial, unblemished by pesticides, insecticides or manmade fertilisers, albeit littered with unexploded ordnance. Over the past several decades, war had made farming a risky endeavour, but with peace and an abundance of rich soil the limited size of the farms we were passing struck me as odd. Most were subsistence sized; small patches that could hardly feed a family. I wondered why weren't the returning Sudanese clearing land by the acre, planting seeds and reaping the benefits of a lush and fertile land?

One answer lies in the psychology of war. People who have lived most of their lives accustomed to the vagaries of conflict don't plan for the future. Why plant more than you need if you won't be there to harvest the fruits of your labour? I couldn't argue with the logic but wondered how long it would take before the mindset changed, how many years of peace would give enough comfort to people to plan for their future.

We passed small hamlets, speeding by and leaving a long trail of dust in our wake. Children ran out of clusters of thatched huts waving before dropping out of sight. Other than the road we were travelling on there was little to distinguish today's South Sudan from what explorers, missionaries, and colonialists saw a century or more ago. *In The Heart of Africa: Three Years Travels and Adventures in the Unexplored Regions of Central Africa from 1868 to 1871*, Dr Georg Schweinfurth describes the area much as I saw it that day: 'No regular towns or villages exist throughout the…country. The huts, grouped into little hamlets, are scattered about the cultivated districts, which are separated from one another by large tracts of wilderness many miles in extent.' A half century of wars on the back of a century of colonial neglect had preserved this land as it was when Dr Schweinfurth had visited in the mid-nineteenth century.

The drive took longer than I had hoped. The first hour was pure bliss, watching the scenery passing by from an open-top vehicle. By the second hour the cramped quarters and dust from the lead vehicle made the journey tedious. During the third hour my muscles were sore and as the fourth passed it was simply painful.

By the time we made it to Mundri, night had long fallen and I had no idea where I was going to sleep. In general, I try to avoid arriving to new places at night, especially rough neighbourhoods, war zones or, in the case of Mundri, a regular venue for tribal clashes. But I had no choice so I fumbled with my pack in the dark and with no street lamps to guide my way I walked to the first group of people I could spot to ask them where I could spend the night.

I'm not sure what they thought of the white guy, dumped on the side of the road by a group of soldiers, asking about accommodation. Nevertheless, a finger pointed me across the road to a restaurant. Crossing the main strip running through the centre of Mundri, a dirt road like all other roads, literally every other road, in rural South Sudan, I entered the huddle of people in front of the supposed lodge. There was no sign out front, no reception room, no indication at all of any sort of accommodation. Instead, I saw a few people sitting on the dirt escarpment that would serve as a storm water drain in a few weeks' time as the rainy season was fast approaching. A fire was crackling in the centre of another huddled group sitting on plastic chairs staring at a few river fish sizzling in a pan. A bunch of bubbling pots was being tended to by a third group under the single storey building's patio. I approached the least intimidating group, the cooks working the pots under the patio, and asked once again about accommodation. Again, I was pointed onwards, inside this time, towards a room fenced off by chicken-wire. Here I met Sapan. As soon as his hand reached out to welcome me and his wide smile beamed under the florescent lighting, my trepidation dissipated and I felt at ease.

My room for the night was a hut in the backyard. As it cost less than five dollars a night I couldn't complain. It had lights powered by Sapan's generator but no switch to turn them off. The thatched roof seemed to be home to a few bugs, spiders and other assorted creatures, but there was a mosquito net covering the bed, separating my zone from theirs. I left them in peace, hoping they would extend the same courtesy to me. As far as amenities, there were two communal latrines out the back alongside another pair of cubicles meant for washing with hot water boiling in a 44-gallon drum over an open fire. I decided this would be good enough for the next few nights.

I re-joined Sapan for a small meal of rice and river fish after I had washed the dirt from my face and changed into some clean clothes. We quickly got to talking about life in South Sudan. Like so many other educated South Sudanese he had applied for work with the UN mission, the certainty of a regular pay cheque being far more appealing than the hotelier business—a business that didn't seem to be doing too well. He described to me the Mundri version of a financial crisis and his opinion on the root cause.

'I have three huts out of thirteen occupied. Business is not good. The problem is that people are not moving from place to place. The government is spending all of its money in Juba and so there is no reason for people to move through Mundri since there is no money or work in the smaller towns.' This was true enough. Still, I thought that as an entrepreneur Sapan should make the most of whatever the situation, which in my mind he clearly hadn't.

'Why don't you put up a sign in front of the lodge to catch the interest of whoever is passing by?' I asked since I had no idea it was a lodge when I was looking for a place to stay. I had seen other signs as I was driving with the soldiers so it wasn't a new or unusual concept. Some of the signs even had lighting.

He quickly responded by saying, 'I have a sign,' and led me to the back where, true to his word an unblemished sign was leaning against a wall. The words 'Wakil Allah Guest House, PO Box, Mundri West County' were printed with a few rough, hand-painted huts conveying the same message for the illiterate.

I was reluctant to ask the obvious question but ventured anyway. 'Why don't you put the sign on the main road so that people can see it?'

'We don't have a post office box number yet and so the address on the sign is not complete. I can't put it out until it's complete.' It was late at night, I was tired, and so I left the discussion at that. Maybe I'd try the next day to convince him to 'store' the sign at the front of the building, on the road, instead of at the back.

As I crawled under my mosquito net that night I thought about the soldiers who had spent their entire lives at war without access to education, about Abdi who couldn't organise himself if his life depended upon it, which it did, and Sapan who hadn't thought about putting the sign out to let people know that his house was a lodge. What they had in common was that they were all under thirty; they represented the future of this young country.

This is the greatest challenge facing South Sudan—human capital. It's a challenge at the small business level where Sapan and Abdi compete against businesses run by Ugandans, Tanzanians, and other east Africans. Their future seems bleak as the foreigners come with capital and business experience, quickly crowding out the locals. It's also a problem in government. By the time of my second assignment to Sudan, the country had been at war for over twenty years. The people who'd earned the right to fill new positions and reap the benefits of ministerial postings, county administration officials and other jobs were excellent soldiers and commanders but poor managers and administrators. History is short on examples of revolutionaries making a successful shift into the bureaucracy. It would be a long road ahead for these young people and their young nation.

South Sudan wasn't alone. The international community sent an army of bureaucrats and specialists to support the development of the country, including the building of the government's capacity to govern. The list of acronyms adorning the sides of the 4x4s that passed me as I waited stranded by the side of the road was an alphabet soup of organisations, each with its own mandate and mission, bureaucracy and budget. They had already left their mark with highly visible projects scattered throughout the countryside. More development had occurred in the previous few years than South Sudan had seen in half a century. Four years earlier when I was last in Mundri, during my second posting in Sudan and working for CHF International, I crossed the River Yei in a rusted metal boat manoeuvred by a man pulling a rope tied to the other bank. In its place now stood a single span truss bridge built by the World Food Programme connecting Mundri to Lui, its sister town across the river. The local administration building that CHF had built stood proudly in the centre of town, and the land mines that had reduced roads around Mundri into thin slivers of safe passage were slowly being removed. The pressing and often unasked question was not whether the international community could build bridges and roads, but what would be left a decade later.

For many these questions bring about a sense of deja vu. Hadn't we already built bridges and roads? For each generation of Western aid workers, civilian officials or military personnel who eagerly take their jabs for yellow fever and rabies, packing their anti-malaria tablets alongside a copy of Joseph Conrad's *Heart of Darkness*, hope springs eternal. But a closer look at the history of development in Africa, a subject thoroughly discussed and dissected, shows that much of what today passes as cutting-edge development has been tried before in one form or another. Dambisa Moyo's *Dead Aid* along with many other books trace a trajectory of aid projects through the past several decades that begins with a focus on large infrastructure projects in the nineteen fifties and sixties. Poverty alleviation and service provision was the focus in the seventies, as many African countries were suffering from a global recession brought about by the rising price of oil. As interest rates rose on the back of the 1979 oil shock, the eighties saw a period of desperation where African leaders sought concessional loans from multilateral institutions such as the World Bank to keep them afloat. In exchange for these loans, structural reforms such as taxation reform, privatisation of government assets, and changes to social security were required as a quid pro quo. These created social upheaval and considerable pain. By the year 2000 (when I became involved in the aid industry) the new trend was empowerment. Whether it was a focus on democracy, women's rights, or south-south development, the old days of Westerners making the decisions on behalf of the people were thought to be gone. Yet this is proving just a façade. Western politicians who control the finances decide where the money will be allocated, and for transparency and accountability purposes donor government appropriations require strings to be attached—in other words, the money is to be spent for a particular purpose, it will be reported in a particular way, and it will be implemented by a particular group chosen by the donor. This fig leaf of autonomy means that the promise of empowerment is limited, only as sincere as the system will allow, which in most cases is no further than the making of minor decisions.

Having spent a large portion of my life living in developing countries I know that plans don't amount to much. You can start the day with a schedule, but anything from a flooded river to newly identified unexploded ordinance exposed by recent rains will wear down even the strictest of time keepers. Further conspiring against planning are the potholed roads that are rendered inaccessible by only a few hours of rain but can delay a planned visit by days or even weeks.

Without a schedule I decided to begin my first day in Mundri by chasing down some of the local community groups we had supported nearly five years earlier. It was through them that microloans were disbursed, youth were trained, business groups established, and training conducted. The program we had run in this isolated corner of South Sudan was a multi-million dollar project billed as a livelihoods and local governance project. In addition to the community focused components, we were constructing county administration buildings for officials who were otherwise running their affairs under trees or in huts. All in all, it was a significant challenge in terms of logistics, but an even harder developmental conundrum.

The logistics meant that driving to the site from the nearest sizeable airport took at least eight hours during the dry season, many more during the wet. Construction materials had to be purchased and transported from Uganda as there was no market for such supplies in the area. Skilled workers were in short supply, so we had to train apprentices or bring them in from other areas since the local community around Mundri had only recently started to return from the safety of the bush or the displaced persons camps.

From a developmental perspective, the issue was the common challenge of balancing donor expectations with sustainable outcomes. Were we low-cost construction contractors with experience working in war zones tasked with building a structure to improve governance? Or should we have been responding to the needs of the community by strengthening local capacity? This would mean buying locally but paying higher rates for materials, building construction skills by sending people on appropriate training programs, or ensuring apprenticing was occurring. All of this would lead to considerable delays. Both are legitimate approaches, each with their own strengths and weaknesses.

Yet the decision wasn't up to the community, to the specialists I employed, or to me. The money we had received for this grant was from the United States Office of Foreign Disaster Assistance, whose mandate is 'saving lives, alleviating human suffering, and reducing the social and economic impact of disasters', while the next office along in the chronology of development, the Office of Transitional Initiatives, is the one tasked with 'helping local partners advance peace and democracy [by providing] short-term assistance targeted at key political transition and stabilisation needs.' Having received money from OFDA rather than OTI meant that our contracts were shorter, limited in scope, and bound

No Dancing, No Dancing ~ 23

by measures of success that were formulated so they could feed into OFDA's global indicators of success. We needed to save lives and alleviate human suffering, not help local partners. So we went for the logistical nightmare that would lead to finishing the job quicker at the expense of building local markets, supply chains and trades skills, but where we could do our best to balance the two competing demands.

Armed with a copy of the project's final report, I set out looking for the New Sudan Women's Federation, one of the few local groups we engaged with. The urban centre of Mundri has, I was told, about ten thousand residents, and is less than an hour's walk from one end to the other, yet no one I asked had heard of the organisation. I enquired with shop owners, a war veterans' association, and officials at the local administration offices. It was becoming disconcerting. Had the group folded? Were they a pop-up organisation that appeared when funds were available and disappeared when money had run dry? Just as I began to worry that I wasn't going to find anyone who could help me, I ran into a team from Oxfam. I approached them, as I had a half a dozen others, assuming that they were from the area and asked if they knew where the Women's Federation was. They didn't, but they did know of the Mundri Women's Association. This was good enough for me, as I was sure they would know the whereabouts of their competitors. So I followed the directions and eventually found their offices.

Sure enough the women at the Association knew of the Federation, but they told me that the director, Susan Pormeli, whom we had worked with, had just given birth two days ago. She wouldn't be at the offices but most likely at home.

'Do you want me to take you to her home?' asked Esta, a program officer with the Association.

I wasn't quite sure about the etiquette around post-natal situations, but I thought I'd just follow my new guide's lead. Needing a car to get to Susan's house, we climbed into Abdi's jerry-rigged Honda (he'd turned up late the night before after having figured out that the problem was a hole in the fuel tank) and began to wind our way through the suburbs of Mundri. Navigating around small gardens and mango trees, the road eventually came to an end in a small, beautifully tended clearing surrounded by a group of adobe brick huts and small gardens—the African equivalent of a suburban cul-de-sac. I politely stayed back admiring how dirt surfaces could be kept so clean and tidy while Esta went looking for Susan. This wasn't the first time or place that I had seen women bent over parallel sweeping hardened earth with bundled straw, but it never ceases to amaze me how they manage to keep it so smooth and clean.

Dressed in a red sleeveless top and a flowing orange patterned sarong, Susan welcomed me to her home, kindly offering a wooden chair in the shade of a mango tree. I had heard of how tough Sudanese women were, but the thought of giving birth two days earlier and then having the energy to entertain a stranger's questions was impressive. When I was living in Wau, capital of Western Bahr al Ghazal state and the next stop on my journey, I was told of a pregnant woman who had made for the privacy of the walled vacant block beside our compound. Apparently, she gave birth and then continued along her way. I wasn't quite sure if this was a true story, but I couldn't imagine that the staff would have made it up.

I could see that Susan wasn't chirpy, but she was determined to meet with me and carry out her duties in representing the organisation. So I decided to continue, but not before asking about her newborn, her fourth child, whom she had named Jacinta. 'She is well, but she will be the last one,' Susan assured me with a certainty in her voice that made me believe her.

The New Sudan Women's Federation was established in 2002, becoming a major partner of our operations in 2005. They were organisers and managers of the small group-lending microfinance pilot program that we had initiated as well as activists against sexual and gender-based violence. I was eager to hear about how both of these programs had panned out as they represented the less visible and tangible elements of aid, yet had a tremendous potential to effect change.

Susan was particularly proud of their work with gender-based violence in rural communities: 'We worked with community elders to develop a code of conduct that the community signed. It was then put where all could see, sometimes on a mango tree or wall,' she told me in the melodic voice that I associate with east African women. 'Some participants started to realise that violence against their women was not good. Some of the men even came and asked that we do the training again.'

'Do you remember what was included in the code?' I asked.

'Sure, I helped develop it,' she explained, outlining the details. I later found a copy of the code, which reflected her recollections:

Code of Conduct

This code of conduct serves as a guide to prevention and response to gender based violence in communities of Amadi, Mundri, Kotobi and Lozoh payams. It refers to the way the community leaders and members should behave in order to combat gender based violence right from the grassroots levels. It is a moral code and doesn't have force of law.

1. Be a role model to the community members by practicing nonviolent behaviours or things that contribute to violence such as excessive drinking.
2. Inform members of the community to be aware of the dangers and consequences of gender based violence using all possible means including community meetings.
3. Enlighten community members to give their children, boys and girls equal opportunity and treat them in the same manner, overloading girl child with domestic chores impedes the development and causes a high rate of female school drop outs.

4. Discourage growing, selling and smoking of opium (bangi) and excessive drinking in the community. The influence of these substances makes people to be violent.
5. Ensure widow inheritance is done with full consensus of the two parties' man and woman.
6. Discourage the practice of paying high dowry as this is one of the contributing factors to domestic violence. In addition it is preventing young people from getting married on time.
7. Handle cases of gender based violence sensitively. Ensure reported cases of gender based violence are treated with respect, confidentiality and ensure the security of the survivor when needed.
8. Encourage community members to report cases of gender based violence to the police, chief or administrator. Such cases include forced early marriage, domestic violence, forced wife inheritance, rape etc.
9. Follow up on reported cases to ensure all possible appropriate actions are taken. This includes making sure the survivor receives all the possible required assistance; the perpetrators are punished, and the punishment is equivalent to the damage.
10. Encourage women members of the community to participate in income generating and other empowerment activities to reduce the dependency of women and lead life with security and dignity.

'Did it change the behaviour of men in the community?' I asked.

'Most men would listen, other than the drunks. They thought we wanted to spoil their wives,' she responded.

'What about now, are they still using the code, are you still training communities?' I asked as I was eager to hear of progress or just some sort of continuation.

'The old chiefs have gone,' she replied flatly. 'There is a new administration, so the code of conduct hasn't been in use since 2008. When CHF funding stopped, activities stopped since we didn't have money to transport trainers into the rural areas and there was no money to provide food during the workshops.'

What an enormous pity this was. Gender-based violence in South Sudan was a major problem that would continue to grow worse as soldiers returned home without a job but with access to cheap alcohol. The project had hit the right spot, tackling the right issues and making the all-important first entry into a community, but was met with no follow up, no expanded programming, nothing. I couldn't blame the donors this time. The fault lay with us. What separates NGOs from contractors, making them a preferred vehicle of delivery for community development, is that they can commit to a locality for the required long term, sometimes a decade or more. They do this by bidding on various contracts, as would a business, but in addition drawing upon general fundraising to cover the financing gaps, ensuring that the core operational team can survive even when new funding is hard to come by. This mode of operation, though, was being challenged by not-for-profit contractor models that had no fundraising capacity and in effect functioned as any other company would, just without turning a profit. CHF was one such group, with the result that when our contract with OFDA ended, so did our presence.

It was nearing lunch time, so I asked Susan about the microfinance program, knowing that some of the women had set up restaurants with their loans. She recommended Lucia's bread-and-beans restaurant as a place to have lunch and meet one of the borrowers. Lucia's bread-and-beans wasn't the actual name of the restaurant. It didn't appear to have a name, no one seemed to refer to it by any name other than 'Lucia's' and its location—just off the main road across from the bus station, which isn't really a bus station but rather an open patch of land.

There are many different variations of microfinance. In places where the rule of law has influence, microfinance often resembles traditional borrower-lender relationships where any breach of contract is enforced in the courts. In places such as South Sudan where traditional law dominates and the court systems are still in their infancy, peer pressure serves as collateral. I asked Susan about the details of their pilot lending program.

'When we gave them that money they had to return it after six months. But they paid it in instalments with five per cent interest.'

'How often were the instalments?' I asked, knowing the response as I had read it in the report but also aware that our reporting didn't necessarily always match the reality on the ground.

'Every month they used to give something at the end of the month. Each group had ten women, some of them didn't receive and some of them received money. After those returned back the money, they then gave to another woman and another woman.' This was the essence of group lending. On paper the concept was that ten women would get together while only five or six would receive a loan. As the money was returned it would then go to other women in the group who hadn't received it the first time. If the original borrowers defaulted, the other group members suffered, so peer pressure and group support reinforced success.

'So what happened to the capital? Does NSWF still have the original money?' I asked. It would have circulated many times over by now if it had been managed well, reaching hundreds if not thousands of women.

'By that time, they tell us, let us give that money to those women.'

I wasn't sure that I had grasped what she meant so I clarified: 'So some women had to return the money with interest, but then CHF told you for those that did not return it to keep it? Is that right?'

'Yeah.'

'How many times did you lend it out before CHF said "just give it to them"?'

'We give it to them two times or three times.'

I couldn't figure out what had happened here. It was only a pilot project so the amount of money involved was insignificant, but the message that such a decision sent to the borrowers and to NSWF was corrosive to long-term development. The next time a microfinance provider came to the area, word would have already gotten around that if you're the last one in line you'll get to keep it all.

I saw that Susan wasn't feeling well, but stoically she brushed it off saying that she only had a small headache.

'If it's okay with you I just have one more question and then I will move on,' I said. 'What type of activities does your organisation currently do?'

Susan responded weakly, whether out of embarrassment or exhaustion, I wasn't quite sure: 'We don't do much now. We get funding from headquarters for legal training of paralegals and some adult literacy. But we are waiting for a new donor to continue our activities.'

Despite being bitterly disappointed I had to thank my two guides, so I decided to treat Abdi and Esta to lunch at Lucia's. After our goodbyes with Susan and a short drive back to the main road, we quickly found the restaurant. It wasn't a restaurant per se, more like an open shed serving food. Lucia had built a corrugated iron structure using tree branches for columns, hard-packed dirt for the floor, and a few colourful plastic chairs and wooden tables for furniture. The place contained three men sipping soft drink when we arrived. Lucia was bent over the stove preparing some dough. She had a wraparound sarong that she would readjust regularly and a loose fitting t-shirt. I was struck by her age—she appeared to be at least fifty—having assumed that the entrepreneurs of this scheme would be young adults.

I asked Lucia for one of whatever she had ready. As it turned out the dish of the day was *foul*, a Middle Eastern and North African dish of beans, which interestingly she served in a thick peanut paste. Tomatoes, onions, and buffalo meat were served as an accompaniment to the dish. I hadn't tasted foul with buffalo meat before—it tasted great.

I asked Lucia how much money she had received from the New Sudan Women's Federation and whether it had been enough to establish herself.

'That money I received from the group was $100 and I used it to start this restaurant. But that money was too small. I cook from early morning into the night and I can only afford to send two children to school.'

'How many other children do you have?' I asked.

'Three more. They have finished sixth grade and are now working collecting firewood that they sell in the market.' She responded through Esta's translation. 'With $300 or $400 I could have opened a small market selling sugar or flour that I buy in Uganda and be able to make enough money to send them all to school.'

A few hundred dollars more would have made the difference between being able to continue to educate all five children and sending them to earn a meagre living after sixth grade. A few hundred dollars was about half of my monthly phone bill when I was working in Khartoum as the country director. In the budget supporting the sexual and gender-based violence program run out of our offices, the one that had helped Susan develop the code, $146,000 out of a budgeted $210,000 went to costs associated with the expatriate specialist.

We had rushed in to undertake activities that looked good when reported to a donor, activities that ticked Western cultural trend-setting boxes of microfinance and gender and then left, patting ourselves on the back. Five years later the leaders trained in dealing with gender based violence were no longer leading, the staff trained as trainers were no longer training, and the women borrowers interested in building on their credit record could not borrow as there was no capital left.

As I returned to my hut I thought about our work with local groups. I didn't want to brush it all aside based upon just one organisation's challenges, so I went back to the project documents to see who else had been a partner.

The Mundri Youth Development Association offices could be seen from the main road lying opposite the bus station and behind one of the largest mango trees I had ever seen. These iconic trees, ubiquitous throughout South Sudan, are tall and robust with a beautiful symmetry that makes them appealing to the eye. They're the Swiss knife of African trees, offering shade from the sun, shelter from the rain, food for the hungry, medicine for the sick, meeting place for the busy, and a marker for the lost. In 2003 I spent the better part of a week lying on a simple steel-framed bed under one of these magnificent trees in Raga, near the border with Central African Republic, getting to know it intimately while recuperating from a foot infection. The swelling had taken a turn for the worse, with a Red Cross doctor musing about amputation. Instead, I placed my faith in a university educated Sudanese doctor, who gave me the largest pills I had ever seen and told me to take one three times a day for five days, which I did, with obvious difficulty. About four days had passed, and with little change in my situation I went to see a missionary sister who I'd heard had a medical background. As I presented my medication and she looked over my foot she simply giggled. Embarrassed by the situation, she explained to a female friend of mine in French that I had been prescribed vaginal suppositories. A few days of the sister's cocktail of drugs and I was able to hobble around again. After a week under the mango tree I flew out of Raga. Days later the town was attacked, precipitating an exodus of tens of thousands of people including my local staff, who began their month-long march north to a temporary camp I helped set up in Al Fardos, having avoided, through luck, being swept up in the mayhem.

Zakaria Wisely is the director of MYDA, a grassroots association with over a hundred paying members. I found him sitting behind his desk in the three-room offices of the association while a few other young boys were working away at a set of computers in the front room. He was enthusiastic to meet with me and eager to reminisce about the CHF team he had worked with even though he wasn't the director at the time. Focused on the question of sustainability, I asked Zakaria what he thought was the benefit of our contribution to the association.

'We have an office now,' was the simple and obvious answer.

I decided to change tack and asked instead, 'What services does MYDA offer to its members?'

'Based on that computer training CHF gave to MYDA we now have seven trainers who teach members to use the computer.' I walked around to look at the equipment. Of the three computers sitting in the front room, one was broken and none of the solar powered battery packs worked.

'Do you offer any other benefits to your members?' I asked.

Zacharia just shrugged, saying, 'The purpose of the organisation is to end poverty.' A noble cause but I wasn't quite sure we had helped in reaching it.

There was a third local organisation with whom we had partnered, but I doubted the story would be any different. Resigned to the fact that our support had not lasted much beyond our direct funding I decided to head to my hut. I strolled past the locality's administration building that CHF had constructed. It was standing tall, full of people and activity, a substantial improvement on the previous open air offices. Five of these had been built, constituting the main component of the project. Additionally, several thousand agriculture tools and seeds were distributed, which I presume proved useful. Should we have simply stuck to constructing buildings and handing out gifts? Obviously the international community was good at this, but the history of development is replete with examples of construction projects unused and left decaying due to a lack of funds, skills, or experience in maintaining them. Handouts, such as the tools and seeds, are not much better as they're often bulk purchased, providing a general solution without knowing each individual's needs and, as is true anywhere in the world, gifts that aren't earned aren't valued. Having visited the projects, it was time to engage with the community leaders.

In South Sudan the layers of administration begin at the village level, known as the boma. The chief of the boma is the head of a council of village elders and presides over the local community. In Lui the chief of the boma, Aliyaza Bilyali Dawood, had been in his position since 1975. Aliyaza became chief during the short period of peace after the first civil war and then continued to lead his people as the second war broke out in 1983, moving with them as the front lines shifted for the next twenty-two years of fighting.

Our meeting was held in a small administration office in Lui together with a few others who had decided to join in the conversation, including Scopas May Yaramas, the boma administrator, and an articulate young man named Paul Doctor who offered to translate if needed.

The chief was a thin man with a salt and pepper beard that hung from his jaw. Aliyaza didn't abide by a particular dress code to identify himself as a chief. Instead he wore a white t-shirt, a pair of well-worn brown pants and flip-flops, slouching in his chair, looking at ease and vaguely disinterested. Although I couldn't see it, I was sure that he had a chief's stick, the main emblem of authority for a man in his position. These walking sticks are beautifully carved from ebony and ivory, eye catching and telling of the authority the holder carries.

Explaining my background, I began by asking the chief which foreign aid organisations had delivered the best results for his community. Without asking the chief, Paul responded: 'Samaritan's Purse.' The boma representatives murmured in ascent. I wasn't surprised by the answer; this evangelical group had arrived in 1997, revived the hospital, built an additional wing including a children's unit, and continued to expand the capacity of the health services in the area for the next ten years.

Paul continued by adding, 'They came with a certain set time frame with them. That time frame ended, they went back to

America. This does not mean the community developed a negative attitude towards them.' Quite the contrary, he explained—because Samaritan's Purse had successfully handed over responsibility to the government they were respected. They had trained the staff, equipped the hospital, developed outreach teams that engaged with villages, and ensured that the system was sustainable by transitioning ownership to the government only once it had the resources and expertise to take control.

Moving on to current issues I asked the chief, 'Since the war is over and there is a government in place, what should foreign organisations be doing now?'

This time Paul conveyed the question and translated the chief's response: 'The expectation for any international organisation is not just to come and sit. They have to learn an example from organisations like Samaritan's Purse. When CHF, left they left nothing here, they only left the carpenters.' His criticism was not of the carpenters that we had trained, but that from all of the activity, the compound, visiting expatriates, vehicles and staff, the carpenters were the only evidence of self-reliance left behind.

I didn't expect the chief to be aware of everything that CHF had done, but considering we were sitting ten metres away from a bakery established by CHF I would have thought he'd have mentioned it. I found out later that it was only intermittently operational and so understood his omission.

The chief continued, 'If any organisation is to come here, the priority is to strengthen local people so that they can realise their potential to mobilise their own resources and sustain themselves. They also need to make some structures so that it can be permanently realised that they did this, because people here believe in remembering old histories through buildings and other things that can be maintained for long.' This explained the signs that seemed to be posted everywhere. There were signs recognising the work of organisations long gone on structures converted into other uses, but the signs stayed behind. The South Sudanese community used signs like Western societies use memorials, to remember important events and people of the past.

'When CHF left, the name of CHF is not heard here any longer. It is forgotten, because they did not leave anything concretely,' the chief added without softening the blow.

I asked what he meant by 'concretely'; did it include training?

'Realise their potential,' he said, enunciating each word slowly and clearly, as if it held some sort of magical meaning. 'Either you train them vocationally or academically, but help them realise their potential.'

I understood that the chief's focus was on the village. His responsibilities didn't reach as far as the administration buildings we had built for the counties, utilised by officials two administrative levels above his. So I asked, 'It looks like there were some successes and some failures. Why do you think that some CHF projects failed?'

'Bad community relations,' he said without hesitation. 'The expatriates brought staff from Eastern Equitoria [another state in South Sudan] who didn't adapt to the situation and local area. They only employed one watchman and one driver from Lui.'

I had known about this issue. The problem was one of expediency; we had an eighteen-month grant from the US government. Eighteen months to set up operations in an inaccessible corner of one of the more inaccessible countries on one of the most inaccessible continents. By the time satellite communications were up, rudimentary housing established and outreach to the community and government completed, the program was nearly half over. There wasn't time to hire locally, provide training, and develop a local cadre of capable hands to lead. I didn't try these excuses on the chief—not because he wouldn't understand but because he expected results and we hadn't delivered. That was all that mattered.

The handouts such as tools, seeds, and construction activities had been well received, but part of our responsibility was to transition away from handouts and encourage self-reliance. In South

Sudan the international community had rushed in to provide aid during the conflict when human suffering was at its peak, and by all accounts both countries succeeded in their responsibilities. As the fighting subsided and the humanitarian crises passed, the aid industry was supposed to, at least on paper, transition away from lifesaving support to longer-term development by adopting transitional programming—small-scale activities that should grease the wheels of long-term development as it rolls into town. This did not occur as planned. Transitional programs such as the one in Mundri/Lui clearly required long-term commitments, but were hampered by short-term contracts and donor expectations of immediate, quantifiable results. Returning to South Sudan five years after the transitional program was expected to have paved the way for long-term projects, I found none. There were some projects operating through expatriates based in regional centres driving in for a day and then returning back to the sanctuary of their compounds. But these projects were mainly focused on building the capacity of the government. But gone were the projects that worked to strengthen communities from within the community, helping people to help themselves instead of relying upon the government. These projects had ended as quickly as they had come, ours being the last in the area.

It was late in the day as I headed to a dinner appointment with the Oxfam team I'd bumped into earlier. I had asked if I could meet with them to talk about their perspectives on community development and they responded by inviting me to dinner.

We met at their accommodation—a star or two above the hut I was staying in. Sitting across from me at the single white plastic garden table that the lodge provided as a social corner was Abdulrahman Wandati, a Kenyan consultant for Oxfam, and beside him was Jonas Anwa, Oxfam's area representative.

Abdulrahman spoke with an academic's air and a clipped accent. He was as intellectually impressive as his English was old fashioned, using words and phrases such as 'behove' and 'if you will' that only seem to have survived in former British colonial outposts. Jonas was more reserved, less comfortable with industry jargon, but very familiar with the challenges facing his country.

I explained to them the journey I had undertaken and my latest thought: 'It seems to me that some community groups in South Sudan are fronts operating as contractors under the guise of having community support, popping up when donors come with money then retreating back into hibernation. They are not representing the people's voices but rather the dictates of the international community and their own interests.'

'You've raised a very interesting point,' Abdulrahman responded. 'It's very rare that small community organisations operating in the rural areas would do advocacy; they will do welfare, self-help, or a water project without questioning why there wasn't any water there in the first place.'

'Indeed,' he continued as if he'd known my questions in advance and had prepared, 'the classical civil society ought to be a people's organisation. It ought to be mitigating on behalf of the people against the excesses of the government and market. The reason I'm slightly lenient to the civil society organisations in South Sudan is because of their journey, their historical journey. To a large extent a good number of today's civil society organisations once actually existed as a social arm of the struggle movement. They have not transited properly; they have not shed off the previous identity and adopted a new identity upon which you can now tick them off as being civil society organisations.'

He paused to take a sip of his tea, making eye contact with those listening as though to check that they were keeping up.

'Now comes the question of the egg or the chicken. Should the existing civil society organisations in South Sudan drive the democracy agenda or should there be an imposed incubation of democracy, which then creates a paradigm in which civil society will operate? It behoves us to try to galvanise whatever little democratic awareness there is so that we can start creating the kind of values for which you can talk about democracy. But unless we create those values, that ideology if you will, within which the South Sudanese person who is neither in the government or the market will believe that they matter, even though they have no bank account, even though they hold no political position, then maybe it will be too soon for democracy.'

Abdulrahman's ideas on civil society reflected challenges faced by nation-building efforts worldwide over the past decade. In Afghanistan and Iraq, the West's objective was to establish democracy without taking the time to foster those values that are critical to sustaining democracy.

'You do not plough a lot of resources before you build the capacity for accountability,' he said, referring to local organisations, 'so you start small as you build the structures, especially the structures for absorption [of funds] and accountability.'

As an example, Jonas and Abdulrahman mentioned Oxfam's efforts in Somalia. In the late nineties an Oxfam staff member, Dorothy Apples, went to Somalia and began working with women's groups. As part of her work she integrated into the community, becoming one of the local women. Dorothy spent time interacting with them in their daily lives and building their trust before she started to organise them, bringing them together into loose knit groups to lead change in their communities. At those early stages all that she required from them in terms of accountability for Oxfam funds was proof that activities had happened—no receipts or reports.

'The level of accountability increased to the extent that when we went to train them recently on organisational development they grasped it quickly. Now there is up to one hundred of these groups who can competently handle any project funds given to them by an international donor,' Abdulrahman told me. It took a decade of funding and day-to-day interaction to help develop a small group of women into an effective, transparent, and accountable organisation.

It seemed that the actual work occurring on the ground, the gender-based violence awareness raising, the microfinance lending, and even the youth computer training worked. There was a grassroots-led embrace and a clear demand for the activities. What was causing them to fail were the self-imposed time frames that limited our ability to entrench the gains. It was two steps forward and one step back, largely caused by an aid industry that held a view that presumes resources and training offer an instantaneous solution without considering culture, tradition, and history.

Spaghetti logic

For one of the poorest countries in the world, South Sudan is surprisingly expensive and I was quickly running out of money. Since there are no ATMs, the plan was to bring enough cash to get me through two weeks but not too much to lose sleep over if I was robbed. Back in Juba I counted out what I had left and tried to figure out how I was going to pay for Charles to accompany me to Wau.

Charles is a Sudanese Australian, but before he migrated to Perth to take up citizenship in his newly adopted country he was a locally hired staff member with the IRC. I first met him in 2001 when I arrived at my posting in Wau. He was the administrator of the office and I was the incoming field coordinator.

When I landed in Wau nine years earlier, my first taste of what lay ahead came as the cargo plane touched down and we taxied past the carcasses of crashed or trashed airplanes littered along the side of the dirt runway. Some, like the one I flew in, had bullet holes that would eventually get the better of it; others, such as the one that lay at the end of the runway, over-reached on landing and struck land mines, permanently disabling itself. At the time I was twenty-six years old, stepping into a war zone, knowing no one, and having no training. I was clueless to the risks. And so Charles became my guide.

As a front-line town surrounded by rebels, Wau did not provide much in the form of comfort, but Charles was kind enough to make my residence as welcoming as possible. My home had a meagre generator, which ran for about an hour or two during the day, barely powering the computers, a ceiling fan and a deep freeze. Otherwise there was city electricity a few hours a week—a cause for celebration when it came on. The sole source of water was a well at the Medicin Sans Frontiers compound from which they would kindly refill the water tank sitting on top of my open-air shower. The kitchen was a fire in the backyard, the toilet was a hole in an outhouse, and the furniture amounted to two worn couches, a small coffee table, two steel frame beds and some cupboards, all on a bare cement floor. Due to the security situation there was a curfew at seven pm until seven am.

For the next nine months I lived alone with little social interaction other than during my working hours with Charles and some of the staff—the same people I was now looking forward to meeting once again. Every few days after work or on weekends I'd try to meet up with one of the other seven or eight expatriates living in Wau before I'd scurry back in time for the curfew. The locking of the house's tall metal gates marked the stark transition from a daytime of activity to a nighttime of stillness and solitude. As the gates creaked shut, thoughts of the outside world dissipated. Without electricity I couldn't do any work and without the luxury to walk outside I was forced to occupy myself with the things I could find in the compound. During the early days it felt like a prison cell. On one occasion, I mixed some cement, poured it into two cans used by the World Food Programme to distribute oil, and joined them with a steel tube to make my own gym equipment. As the sun set and birds filled the sky making their final preparations for the evening, I would head straight for a fold-out chair in the walled patch of dirt that resembled a back yard. If there was enough sunlight left in the day I'd read or write, leaving the kerosene lantern and the words of the BBC World Service for the evening. Over time, my quiet compound became a rustic retreat in which I found solace.

While still in Jordan and preparing for my return trip to South

Sudan, I wrote to Charles in Australia to get contact details of our old friends from Wau. He wrote back saying that he was also headed there for the first time since he had left three years earlier. He was arriving a few days after me, so I waited for him in Juba after my return from Mundri. We had agreed to travel to Wau together to see what had happened over the years; he was just as interested to follow up on our work as I was.

As I waited for Charles, a number of people told me that a road trip to Wau would be risky. The temperament of the soldiers and officials in one of the states we'd have to drive through could prove problematic. Nobody was even sure that I'd be allowed to pass, though I had all the necessary paperwork. I couldn't risk losing three days going there and then being sent back, so with regret I ditched my resolution to catch the finer details of the country by sticking to cars and buses. Instead, I headed to a local airline that flew the route from Juba to Wau and counted out the money for two tickets.

Charles arrived in Juba as promised and we spent the entire flight busily catching up. Landing for a stopover in the small isolated town of Aweil brought back harrowing memories of the first time I was there. As the only expatriate from neighbouring Wau with a travel permit for Aweil, I was asked to make a visit. I jumped onto a UN flight that was island hopping between the northern Sudanese controlled towns, each surrounded by the rebels and inaccessible by land as it would have meant crossing the mined and volatile front lines. Word had spread of food shortages affecting the population in this town of twenty-five thousand people. In March 2001, together with Dr Anthony, a South Sudanese doctor who also worked with IRC, I flew to Aweil to find a calamity.

Aweil at the time was surrounded by the Sudanese People's Liberation Army, as was Wau, but where Wau had a buffer of a few kilometres separating the two sides, the front lines in Aweil were a short walk from the edge of town. This led to more than the obvious security threat. With land in short supply farming was a near impossibility, so food had to be flown in, making it beyond the reach of the majority of people. In addition, with a high water table, latrines had to be built above ground, yet there was very little space to empty the faeces and dispose of other refuse so it just piled up in the streets and homes, creating a severe health risk.

As I walked around the small town visiting the burned-out or destroyed buildings (where the poorest often squat) I found children so weak they were unable to swat the flies away from their bodies. They had the tell-tale signs of malnutrition: bloated belly, disproportionately thin arms and legs, and blond or greying hair. Without proper equipment or training, I did what I was instructed to do by our Khartoum-based health coordinator. Taking a tape from my pack I started to measure the middle upper arm circumference of the children and recorded their ages in a notebook. This method is only a rough guide that is used as a rapid assessment tool, but it was enough to confirm that there was a crisis. Meanwhile, Dr Anthony, a general practitioner, spent his time in the hospital where he was roped into performing several surgeries. He later told me that even though he didn't have any surgical qualifications or experience, it was better than leaving the people to die. This was my first time facing the ravages of a famine. A heart-wrenching experience, made still worse because I had little to offer to ease the people's suffering.

After a short break Charles and I were called to board the plane, leaving behind Aweil and thoughts of its past. As we flew above the recently flooded landscape, Charles explained how he had struggled to settle down in Australia. His children loved it but he couldn't find work. His degree from a Sudanese university was given an equivalency of a high school diploma. Having held some relatively senior and well paid positions with an American NGO, he wasn't prepared to go back to studying. Instead, he decided to return to South Sudan and see what business he could rustle up. It was the right time. With oil flowing, peace finding a foothold and independence just around the corner, there was a lot of money to be made. As a well-connected educated Southerner he should stand a good chance of doing well for himself and his family. Plus, Charles had the right temperament; he was outgoing yet respectful, warm and sincere.

As we descended to our destination I kept an eye out for the giant steel carcasses, wondering whether an entrepreneurial soul had taken them for scrap or if they had been left to rot. As it turned out they were still there. The crashed planes were lying on the same dirt runway leading to the same run-down arrivals terminal with only a new temporary tower to show. But there was something very different about the airport this time round. It was the people buzzing around the terminal. Gone were the soldiers refuelling attack helicopters or unloading Chinese-marked cases of weapons. Instead, a safari lodge style bar took up the space, full of foreigners drinking and listening to music waiting to board their flights and get out of Wau.

Samson met us at the airport. He was a former colleague who had managed to find a job with the UN peacekeeping mission as a logistician. Luckily, he had found me a place to stay that fell within my revised budgetary guidelines.

As we drove up to the Sunset Lodge, home for the next five nights, I couldn't help but feel ripped off. In Mundri I was paying five dollars a night in a clean hut with decent ventilation while in Wau a cell with a wasp's cocoon was going for five times the amount. Run by Eritreans, with several women of varying shapes and sizes appearing to be available for evening pleasures, the Sunset Lodge was a reflection of the new Wau. It was the land of opportunity for a wide array of people. Perched on the junction connecting Congo, Uganda, and Kenya to Sudan, Wau was a busy hub with faces from all over Africa mulling about town. Charles and I randomly met two Liberian men who had travelled across Africa to Wau having heard that there was easy money to be made. Women also travelled there to find riches, often recruited from neighbouring states into jobs as cleaners or cooks during the day and prostitutes at night.

While war was no longer a threat in this city, I didn't like the new Wau. The hope of a better life that peace promised to bring didn't seem to be materialising for many South Sudanese. Instead, with little capital to start their own business and no entrepreneurial experience to build one from scratch, they were relegated to the sidelines to watch as wealth poured into the pockets of those who could make the most of the moment. The few Sudanese who were educated chose the security of working with the UN rather than establishing their own business; so too did the leaders of the liberation movement, who eschewed the risks of private business, instead slipping into secure and lucrative government jobs.

The three of us sat for a few hours, joined later by another former colleague, Angelo Une, who had also joined the UN mission. We laughed as we talked about the past, remembering the good things such as the cartoon screenings we'd host for children who would diligently sit in our office during the weekends. But we also remembered the tough times. Moments after learning of the September 11 attacks, I went out into the street and saw my neighbour, a stationery shop owner, handing out sweets in celebration. Even though I didn't like the new Wau, nor appreciate the accommodation and the brazen drunkenness and prostitution, I went to bed content. Wau remained a special place for me. It was here, on the front lines of a war, that I had unexpectedly found peace and contentment.

Thankfully October sits astride the end of the wet season and the beginning of the dry season in South Sudan. The weather wasn't scorching hot nor was there a daily deluge of rain. For our first visit to an old project, Charles and I decided to walk across town, past two sets of new traffic lights, the first in the whole of South Sudan, across the bridge spanning the River Jur and into the largest internally displaced persons camp in Wau, the Eastern Bank Camp.

In 1998, the eastern bank of the River Jur, until then a thinly forested area of mango trees just above the flood plain, became a refuge for tens of thousands of people seeking safety from the conflict. It was also a place to find food, made available by humanitarian organisations. Earlier that year, a long festering division within the rebel movement combined with an unusually long dry season that ended abruptly with floods caused a food shortage and mass displacement. Over a period of several months people drifted in, leaving behind their failing crops and war-ravaged villages. Humanitarian organisations quickly came to their aid, mobilising resources and personnel. For the IRC this meant setting up a primary health clinic and leading on water and sanitation activities.

Nine years earlier, when I arrived as head of the field office, delivering aid or even making a simple visit to the Eastern Bank Camp (then housing seventy-five thousand people) was a laborious bureaucratic process. Every week a new permit was required from the security forces; which sometimes wasn't given or arrived late, allowing for limited visits only. Once the bureaucratic hurdles were overcome, the challenges came from the rebels, now the government, who would raid herds of cattle grazing on the banks of the river. Fire fights with the government soldiers were common and more than a few times aid workers found themselves on the wrong side or in between, waiting out the battle before returning home.

The River Jur is on the outer fringes of the Nile river basin, feeding the White Nile, which flows north to Khartoum. There it joins the Blue Nile and as one river winds its way through Egypt, eventually releasing into the Mediterranean some of the dirt and sediment it had collected from where we stood at that moment. As we walked across the bridge, Charles pointed down to a site alongside the river where the first missionary outpost in the region was established less than a hundred years ago. In a sense it was the first aid mission, a precursor to the new secular religion that has followed in its footsteps, proselytising democracy and the free market.

There's no method to the madness in the Eastern Bank. Plots are varied in size, with some surrounded by tended gardens and others lost amongst overgrowth. One green thumb had ingeniously lined their garden bed with discarded soft drink cans. The paths, some wide enough for vehicles but most only for walking, wove around the camp in a spaghetti logic. Most of the huts were mud adobe with thatched roofs. Gone were the tents that I could remember. Sadly, it quickly became apparent that most of the infrastructure had also gone. I couldn't see any latrines, most of the water pumps were broken, and all of the drainage ditches crucial for keeping the imminent rains from turning into stagnant pools (so attractive to breeding mosquitoes) were blocked or covered over. Even the health clinic that we built in 1999, a six-room brick structure painted white but badly in need of a new coat, was a shadow of what it had been years ago.

'We haven't received any money to maintain the building,' a young medical assistant told us. 'The roof leaks, drugs are low, we don't have a technician for the lab, and we've run out of malaria testing kits.'

We found Chief Angelo Uraya Dut sitting under a mango tree on a plastic chair. The chief's silver beard and faded red baseball cap were all that set him apart from the others, who were dressed in a similar style: the chief wore a short-sleeve shirt that years ago could have had colour but was now a well-worn off-white. His pants were in the same state, and on his feet he wore a pair of flip-flops. As we approached he was huddled in a meeting with another chief, while four other men lounged about in the small, hard packed dirt clearing. One of these men, Abraham Tom, the only one wearing a long-sleeved button up shirt, recognised Charles and introduced himself as one of the former IRC community health promoters. He had worked with IRC through till 2005, when its programs were shut down.

It was midday and the sun was well hidden behind the thick foliage of the mango tree. A breeze blew across the cold waters of the Jur River, making the site a comfortable place.

'Chief Angelo,' Charles began, using a local dialect and just the right degree of formality, 'it's a pleasure to meet you and be with you today. We are both visiting Wau after having worked here on humanitarian projects with the IRC. Denis was the field coordinator in 2001 and I took over from him when he left later that year until 2004. We're here to visit old friends and see what happened to our projects.'

'You're most welcome. We're happy to welcome back friends who helped our people in the past,' Chief Angelo responded and Charles translated for my benefit.

'Thank you. I'm glad to have the opportunity to visit,' I added.

'Were you here when IRC was working?' Charles asked the chief.

'I arrived in 2005 as the peace agreement was signed. Many of the people around us here also came at that time. But we have not received any support since then,' the chief responded, with Abraham interjecting from time to time as it seemed Charles' range of dialects didn't stretch the full tribal spectrum of the group.

'Are there any NGOs working in the camp?' I asked.

'No, the NGOs have gone because there is no emergency. But now is the time we need help, now we need support because we are here to stay. We need support to help begin new lives,' came the response.

'What about the government?' I continued.

'The government claims it has no budget,' the chief said without a tinge of anger or disappointment. 'But a lot needs to be done. There are not even latrines, people shit all around with no care for health.'

'So why don't people build their own latrines?' Just as I said this, my mind flashed back to a conversation I had nine years ago with a group of chiefs on the same topic in the same place. They wanted us to build latrines. I wanted them to do some of the work themselves. They said there weren't any men around to do the work as they were all fighting. I pointed out that every person in front of me in that meeting was a man and they needed to start helping themselves as we weren't going to be there forever. It seems no one saw the peace coming as they presumed we would be there forever.

The post-NGO period that I had anticipated came a lot sooner than most had expected and clearly no one was prepared to take responsibility.

'We don't have the money to buy the slabs and the walls,' Chief Angelo responded.

The quickest and cheapest latrines to build are simple holes in the ground with a cover and some kind of superstructure such as plastic sheeting wrapped around a bamboo frame to provide privacy. From this basic version additional components can make a latrine last years and even lend a level of comfort. Ventilation in the form of a PVC pipe leading up from the pit with a wind vane and opening draws out the smells as the low pressure on the lee side of the pipe sucks up the air. Septic tanks can be added, even two side by side to allow one to dry and then be cleared as the other is in use.

I didn't want to let this go as I wanted to understand why people weren't helping themselves, so I continued: 'I've built latrines using wooden logs, food ration sacks and dirt for the slab. The grass here in the camp can be woven to make the walls. You could do all that for free.'

It took a while for the response to come back. Abraham attempted to explain the point I was making. It wasn't that I was specifically asking him to build latrines but rather why the people weren't helping themselves. Finally, Abraham came back with a response to my actual question. 'My people are worried the government will evict them from their homes. The government has plans to give the Eastern Bank land to the locals. So we are worried about working and spending money and then losing our homes. The better the property the more likely the government is to give it away. So we don't do anything.'

There was nothing to say in response. The importance of property ownership made just as much sense in this camp as it did in the most prosperous city in the West. Renters are unlikely to maintain a property as well as an owner and squatters never invest a cent.

I decided to press on, unable to let go of my sense that their passive resistance was hurting rather than helping. 'What happened to the water pumps?' I asked as I looked around to point at one of the stumps that was all that remained from our previous investment.

'They broke,' one of the men hanging around the meeting chimed in.

'Did WES come to repair those that broke while they were still operating in Wau?' (WES is the Water and Environmental Sanitation Department within the Sudanese government.) While we were drilling the bore holes all those years ago, UNICEF supplied WES with parts, even stocking their warehouse so that they would not be dependent upon the government's budgetary circumstances.

'When they come they dismantle the pump's head and take the parts. They never come back with new parts,' Abraham answered. Since the peace agreement, the new government of South Sudan had taken over the responsibility but clearly they were also not interested. We had trained members of the community how to repair the pumps themselves, but when spare parts were required it was the role of WES with the aid of UNICEF to provide those parts. It was clear that the government was surreptitiously trying to thin out the camp. Maybe this wasn't such a bad idea; it clearly needed to be properly demarcated, plots allocated and infrastructure built, but cutting back on the amount of potable water available wasn't a humane way of doing this.

'How many remain working?' I asked.

'About thirty of the forty-eight in total are broken,' the chief replied resignedly. Perhaps he had seen it all before. Or perhaps being calm and collected was an electable trait, like being slick and telegenic is for Western politicians. All of the chiefs I had met so far seemed dispassionate about the challenges they faced. Maybe they all knew that like so many foreigners that had come before me, I wouldn't do anything, so why bother getting all worked up about the issues?

'So if the conditions are not good and you're not getting any support from the government, why stay? Why don't people go back to their villages?' I asked.

'Most of the people here are urban people. They fled from different towns and villages when the war came to them. They don't have farms to go to. Many are widows. They have nowhere to go,' came back the translated response.

'What about work?' I asked, returning to the theme that had occupied my thoughts as I'd walked through Wau the night before. 'There are a lot of foreign businessmen setting up new businesses. Have the men of this camp tried to find work with them?'

'We don't have relations with them,' answered Angelo simply.

'What about you guys, have you tried to find work with them?' I asked the other young men gathered in our open-air meeting room.

As though in slow motion, the men shook their heads. No one had bothered to try to find work. No one was bothering to dig their own latrines. No one had even bothered to plant any vegetables in their gardens. In 2001 I had been arguing with the village chiefs to start convincing their people to look after themselves. Our aid operations continued for four years after that. No wonder they ignored my appeals. What I should have done was create a plan and have it signed off by my supervisor (and his supervisor) to ensure its application beyond my tenure. The plan could have detailed a strategy to reduce assistance and eventually withdraw from the Eastern Camp. But this wasn't in the interest of the organisation, as it covered its own operating costs through a percentage of income earned. Nor was it a habit of country directors to refuse additional funding as their success was measured against the amount of money raised. Moreover, the donor, the European Commission in this instance, would have simply found another NGO to do its bidding. This was more than the mentality of war affected populations, it was a dependency aided and abetted by the aid industry.

As I was looking towards Charles to indicate that it was time to leave, Chief Angelo asked, 'IRC were here, they worked very hard and built the clinic, dug latrines, drilled wells. Now you see with your own eyes that since then nothing has been done. What are you going to do for us?'

Angelo's question brought into sharp relief an essential truth that his people were failing to grasp: with the new-found rights they had earned also came responsibilities. In Western democracies the people expect services from the government and in exchange the government extracts taxes from the people. This relationship creates an interlocking of vested interests between the concerned citizen and elected government. It struck me that the people of the Eastern Bank, over nearly a decade of aid industry rule, had grown accustomed to a single-sided social contract. I responded by giving the same spiel as I had in 2001 but with little hope that they would take heed of any of my words.

We thanked our hosts and politely took our leave, heading back to town. As we emerged from the trees onto the main road leading into town, I suggested that we pop into one of the local stalls to grab a drink. Once inside the corrugated iron shack and seated on the plastic chairs, I ordered some cool drinks and asked Charles, 'So what do you think? What went wrong?'

'In general, with the hand pumps, there is no maintenance. The clinic, the roof is leaking, also there is no maintenance. Yet, we trained the sanitation workers. We trained the community health workers—even hand pump mechanics. All this is just a waste, they have not done anything with the knowledge that they acquired,' Charles said.

'Is it a waste?' I asked just as much to Charles as to myself. 'We helped them survive during the years we were there, isn't that something?'

'During the project, yes, they worked very well and the things were okay. But now leadership is not there, which probably means that many of our activities will simply wither away and be forgotten.'

'I wonder what we could have done differently. I mean they are not even cultivating the land,' I said, pondering out loud.

'This is their culture. They are pastoralists, they don't farm. In their tribe farming is socially beneath them. Don't forget when we first came the women did not want to use the latrines at all because they thought that they would not give birth. They also believed that they should not shit where their in-laws did. But they learned and so they should learn new skills now.' I'm sure he was thinking about how he had helped himself by first getting an education, then the job with IRC and eventually moving to Australia, all through hard work. He didn't see why these people couldn't do so as well.

Charles' observations reminded me of the challenges we had faced. The residents of the camp, mainly from the Dinka tribe, refused to use the latrines as they wanted to show others how healthy and rich they were by defecating in the open for others to see. We had come a long way to get to the point where the people understood the need for latrines, but now they didn't want to risk their time and resources to build them.

'It seems to me that the lesson is that we should be providing lifesaving support and then nothing after that. Like you said, they're pastoralists,' I mumbled, slouching exasperated in the plastic chair, watching a herd of long horned cattle stroll past the drinks stall.

'What would you do if you had the money now?'

'I would use the money to mobilise the community. You know what we did in Raga, we involved the community through the chief, we did a lot of meetings with them, we learned about them and they learned about the importance of sanitation. We worked with the community so that at the end they should not say this is IRC property and IRC responsibility. They should feel a sense of ownership. Dig their own latrines, this is what they did, they dug their latrines and we provided them with the materials and lining. Like this they can do their maintenance. Because they were involved in construction, but you go there and dig for them and build for them, they don't care, they say this is IRC property.'

We finished our homemade soft drinks and headed back to town. The day still being young, we decided to drop by the offices of the Southern Sudan Relief and Rehabilitation Commission to get their perspective on the state of the Eastern Bank.

On the way to their offices, Charles told me about his successor in Wau, who had hired northern companies to dig latrines in some of Wau's other camps. Administratively it was a quick fix, but it was an approach that undermined development outcomes. It reminded me of how in Iraq an American contractor, DAI, partnered with two Kurdish companies to implement all of their projects country-wide. They would theoretically work with communities to develop a project that would then be implemented by either one of DAI's Kurdish partners regardless of whether it was a Sunni Arab or Shia Arab area. The community would benefit from the product, but any sense of ownership would be lost and most of the profits would accrue to the Kurds—again an administrative quick fix but ultimately counterproductive. India's former Prime Minister, Jawaharlal Nehru, once said that 'it is more important to adopt the right way, to pursue the right means, than even to have the right objectives, important as that is.' I had come across that quote years ago and it had stuck with me as being particularly appropriate to our work. This should be the ethos of development in a nutshell, but regrettably it has become inverted, where now the objective—a pit latrine or a school—is hurriedly pursued as if it is an end of itself. But it is not. The process matters.

* * *

We found the offices of the South Sudan Relief and Rehabilitation Commission (SSRRC) on the outer fringes of town where wooden huts begin to replace stone houses. Someone had been kind enough to donate prefabricated cabins to serve as offices. We entered one of the three cabins and found Matthew Chan, the director of the SSRRC and Peter Nenenbubu, head of the Raga office of the SSRRC. As both men spoke English well, I explained the reason for our visit without Charles translating.

'The SSRRC,' Matthew informed us, 'is the southern government's statutory body responsible for overseeing the actions of foreign agencies involved in humanitarian aid and development.'

It seemed that he was hesitant to give too much away, not sure of our intentions, but we persevered with some questions.

As Peter worked in Raga I asked, 'Did you know of IRC? I had managed a sub-office there while I was in Wau back in 2001.'

'Yes, of course. It was you and the Germans, but then others came. Actually, I recommended to send IRC personnel home after one month, back to Khartoum, as they were too political and pushing their religion. What work IRC did before was good. The health centre is still functional and the beekeepers are doing well. The problem is the people they send, not IRC itself.'

I recalled through the years a Muslim Arab northerner being sent to manage an office in a religiously and racially sensitive Christian African south, an expatriate in Lui who didn't want to shake hands with local people, and the innumerable drunks I'd crossed paths with who would miss full days of work being so intoxicated: the aid workers themselves were often the problem.

Peter continued. 'ACTED [a French NGO] erected signs claiming project accomplishments as their own. But in actual fact it was an area of FAO [UN Food and Agriculture Organisation] not ACTED. We found this out when a delegation from ACTED and FAO came and we asked the farmers and the farmers told me that they got no support from ACTED but only FAO. ACTED didn't even know where they worked!' Both Peter and Matthew clearly had little respect for many of the aid workers who had come to help them.

'Do you see any difference between NGO aid workers and those of the UN or from the churches for that matter?' I asked both of them.

Peter fielded the question again. 'NGOs need to be guided, they are not organised. They do good work, but they need coordination and guidance. The UN, honestly, have personnel issues, some have no human feeling in their heart, no humanity. The churches we trust and are very good, they are successful because they have the right people who stay in the community and understand the community. NGOs and the UN pick anyone to work for them without qualifications.' Although this was an oversimplification of the aid industry, it largely hit the mark.

Thinking back over the past week, I hadn't had one experience with a South Sudanese who'd worked with an international organisation and didn't recall some story of how either idiotic or selfish the expatriates could be. It's not that every aid worker is a walking caricature, it's just that too many are.

Heading back to Cell 3 in Sunset Lodge, I was ruing my decision to come here. In addition to reaffirming every accusation against the aid industry, this trip challenged the sentimental memories that I had developed of my time in Wau. A part of me had hoped to rekindle and maybe relive the utopia—a place where the good guys were clearly distinguishable from the bad guys, each and every aid worker was a competent humanitarian, and everything we did would have a tangible lasting impact. As I trudged home along the main road, heading back to the crackling speakers, eager women, and tables piled high with beers of the Sunset Lodge, I realised that the utopia of the past was nothing but my own naiveté.

The beauty returns

The next day, like every other day of this visit, was clear and sunny, though it didn't reflect my disposition. The night before I had decided to clear the wasp nest from my wall but failed to close a gaping hole in the false ceiling, an oversight that kept me awake as I feared the opening would bring me face to face with a rat that I heard scurrying along the panels.

Breakfast that morning, as with most of the other mornings, was fried dough and tea served fresh from a small corner stall run by a South Sudanese woman and her young children. It was the only place I could find that was owned and managed by a local; all the other restaurants were run by Ugandans or Kenyans. From there I headed to the River Lodge, located alongside the bridge leading to the Eastern Bank camp. I was told that they had an internet café open to outsiders and since there wasn't any other place in town with public internet, I headed over to see whether I could send a few emails.

From the outside the River Lodge wasn't impressive. A wall that was presumably built decades earlier to protect whatever had once stood on the river's edge was in need of considerable repair. There were no signs out front, but as they say of all exclusive locales the world around, those who need to know need no directions. Eventually I navigated past the guard and headed into the courtyard where the vista changed dramatically.

Breakfast was being served. The smell of coffee, sausages and egg hit me hard; a few expatriates dressed in their khakis were sitting on safari chairs under the shade of a tree, laptops open, sipping their freshly brewed coffee while they tucked into their food. As I scanned the space I tried to guess their occupations. In general, the photojournalist jackets go with the UN folks. The preference to have your life ordered and compartmentalised doesn't fit the freewheeling nature of NGO characters. The latter, mainly young or young at heart, are usually dressed in loose fitting casual clothes, eating at local stalls, and doing better than most in learning the language and culture, though I doubted that I'd find them here. The older folks found in expensive restaurants and hotels tend to be the contractors. Wise to the ways of the industry, not willing to give their time away for a pittance, they're there to do a job, nothing more, nothing less.

* * *

The Aid Industry in a Nutshell

International development assistance comprises a kaleidoscope of foreign aid programs. Some are only tangentially associated with development, such as security forces training, others, like debt relief or concessional lending, are implemented with a stroke of the pen. The most visible portion of development assistance is delivered on the ground through intermediaries, including United Nations agencies, NGOs and development contractors—the three tribes of the aid industry.

Along with their own history, territory, traditions and values, each of the three tribes has its own dedicated funding stream. The majority of development funding for United Nations agencies come from either compulsory assessed contributions from states or voluntary contributions by government. For NGOs and contractors funding is secured through competitive tenders for projects or grants from governments. Alongside these government funding streams NGOs and to a smaller degree United Nations agencies access private donors, while contractors draw from non-aid related business activities.

The perceived comparative disadvantage of NGOs, a lackadaisical approach to management and implementation, began to change in the nineties when NGOs embraced corporate practices and business models. Today they have comprehensive external financial audits, abide by international accounting standards, drive a large part of development research and set the advocacy agenda. A number of NGOs are multi-billion dollar enterprises. Approximately twenty INGOs have between 5,000 to 46,000 employees and the development-focused revenues raised by NGOs through private fundraising now exceed those of the entire United Nations system.

The United Nations' humanitarian and development agencies are struggling to find a justifiable role on the ground as vehicles for the delivery of aid largely as a result of a perception of endless bureaucracy. But like most other bureaucracies they began outsourcing much of their work in an effort to cut costs that has in some cases created lean and efficient operational institutions.

The contracting side has been criticised for lacking altruistic ideals, profiteering and being puppets for their clients. Unlike NGOs and the UN for whom, on paper at least, the client is the beneficiary; the contractor's client is the donor. That they remain viable businesses suggests an ability among at least some to continue to deliver results. This has been achieved in part due to the shift to developing the organisational knowledge base including in-house technical units akin to those of NGOs and UN agencies.

***

These men were clearly contractors, paid by donors to strengthen the capacity of the government, to help them establish ministries, draft legislation, train staff, and build offices. They were specialists in their field, well compensated, with resumes stretching to every inhospitable corner of the world.

Yet I couldn't help but wonder how these mainly Western expatriates, who had grown up with modern technologies, could transfer knowledge on how to establish ministries or develop management mechanisms in a place where electricity is limited, few people use a computer and paperwork isn't just a euphemism for bureaucracy but a descriptor for how work is actually done. At one hundred and twenty dollars a night for a tent and substantially more for a room this was quite an expensive lodge. Adding the cost of the flight, insurance and a standard salary, the cost for each of these contractors sipping their coffee would have amounted to at least twenty-five thousand dollars a month.

In the development community there is a small but forceful movement aimed at encouraging trilateral aid as opposed to the traditional bilateral version (which is country to country) and multilateral (where donors fund institutions such as the United Nations who then run projects). Trilateral aid is where donor countries bring developing country specialists to other developing countries. This is something akin to what Oxfam was doing by hiring Abdulrahmanm, who was from Uganda but working in South Sudan. The idea is that specialists in a country that has successfully transitioned are better placed to train a newly transitioning country than people from highly developed states. Regrettably this model is all too rare. I left the River Lodge as they didn't have sufficient bandwidth to support outside users. Instead I reluctantly headed to my next meeting, to yet another local organisation, this time a women's group.

Charles met me at Sunset Lodge with a driver of a three-wheeled covered scooter. Wau, like no other place in South Sudan that I had seen, had been overrun by these buzzing Chinese-made lawn-mower-cum-taxis. While good on a paved road, anywhere else they struggled. Thankfully, that morning the driver brought us safely to the offices of the Women's Development Group.

The building was still being touched up, but it was full of activity. In the main office we found a few young men gently typing away on computers while workmen were plastering the outside walls. Charles asked one of the men at the computer about Marijana and Rabha, women that we'd both known from our days in Wau. We were pointed to another building just recently built in the same compound, a small hall or training room by the look of it.

As we came around the corner there were shouts of glee; the women recognised Charles and I immediately and rushed over to greet us. Marijana Biri was the Executive Director of the group—tall, wiry thin, with plaited hair running back over her head from a high hair line. Rabha Ellis distinguished herself without any accoutrements but through a sharp tongue and a quick answer to just about every question; she was the Deputy Director of the organisation. Alongside these two women sat Regina Edward Dimo, quiet as most accountants I have come to know, and Elizabeth Deng Wal.

They were thrilled to see Charles and he clearly wasn't embarrassed by being the centre of their attention. I didn't interrupt their reunion, for a while listening to them speak in a local dialect about their lives since Charles had left Wau. After a few minutes Charles politely introduced my interest in their work.

'This is an amazing place,' I said with a tinge of excitement returning in my voice after the past few days of disappointment. 'How did you fund all of this?' I asked. But before they could respond I said, 'Wait, wait, wait, I want to hear it all from the beginning.'

Rabha and Marijana led us over to an oblong plastic table beneath a sunny windowsill. Then they began taking turns to explain how their organisation came about.

'In 1998 a group of nine women came together after seeing the suffering of women refugees. We decided to do something to help them. Because we knew that many women go to the forest to collect firewood and men abuse them there, we decided to organise to give them different training so they can have a new income,' explained Marijana.

'Yes, we were a group of nine women. Teachers, working with WOTAP [Women Training and Promotion Association],' added Rabha.

'That's how Women's Development Group was founded on principles of peace building. That's why women of different tribes are all included. We have Jor and Dinka as well as Fertit tribes all working together even if the men fight,' continued Marijana. 'Then in November 2000, before you came here, CARE gave us some support and we grew into one hundred women. That was when we got our first project from the United Nations.'

'Which agency?' I asked.

'It was the Food and Agriculture Organisation. We wrote a proposal to build backyard gardens because women would go back to their farms in their villages but then get raped. We helped them to cultivate vegetables in the camps to earn income without having to go home.'

'Then IRC got involved?' I asked. 'If I remember correctly it was just before I arrived, as Elvira was already running the program.'

'Yes, in 2001 Elvira met with us and helped us to organise properly. We established by-laws, a constitution, made systems and bought stationery. She also helped us register with the government,' Marijana replied.

This was great. Could this redeem a sliver of success from the past? It had been an uninspiring return so far.

'What kind of activities do you run now?' I asked and they proceeded to list them, finishing each other's sentences.

'Currently WDG is implementing "Sustain Peace & Enhancing Livelihoods in South Sudan". Under this project we have different activities...' explained Marijana before Rabha cut her off.

'Farming in which we provide farming equipment for about 1,000 beneficiaries, most of them are women in rural areas. Also, off-farm activity: we provide loans for income generation, grinding mills and nut paste machines to women who form themselves into working groups...'

Marijana returned to lead the conversation, 'We also do peace building. WDG realised that Western Bahr El Ghazal have been at war for a long time, so we formed peace councils in each location consisting of five persons, two women and three men, to mitigate conflict in the community.'

'Also gender issues,' Regina reminded them.

'Yes, we want women to control resources,' Rabha said, taking centre stage once again, 'by providing tools to them and gender equality awareness to both women and men, to enable men to change their mentality which is against gender equality, because in our community women are considered second class citizens. We also encourage women to work together with men and to find more opportunities for women in decision making, such as the peace councils where men can see the important role of women in peace building. They really have recognised the important role of women among them!'

(Later I learned that the group was very active during the subsequent referendum on independence held in January 2011. Their organisation was a focal point for election monitoring in their state, Western Bahr El Ghazal, deploying 192 observers during the vote.)

'So how did all of this come about? Are you still funded by donors and dependent upon them for covering operational costs?' I asked.

Rabha responded: 'After the support of CARE and winning the FAO project, we partnered with IRC and got a $22,000 grant to help develop programs that created income for WDG. We started handicrafts, embroidery and vegetable gardening, which all helped raise funds. Then in 2006 Oxfam gave us equipment. At the moment all of our funds come from donors but we are transitioning to a sustainable structure. Our plans are to operate as seed merchants, buying seeds from IDP farmers and selling to others as well as working on microfinance. We already started on this with three hundred loans at ten per cent interest over six months.'

The Women's Development Group clearly wasn't just a front, active when funds were available but otherwise dormant. It had a membership of one hundred and sixty women each paying a fee of two Sudanese pounds, not a great deal but a nominal sum that ensured they received some sort of income as well as being a truly membership-based group.

This was the story I wanted to hear. A truly community-based group with a sustainable revenue stream pushing for social change at a pace that met their cultural norms while contributing to the critical moments of their country's transition. The experience of WDG was similar to the Somali groups Oxfam had supported, both being engaged over a longer time frame and receiving different types of support by the international community.

Buoyed by the conversation, Charles and I decided to walk back to Sunset Lodge. The sun was setting, making the otherwise dull yellow sand a beautiful golden hue, the sky was full of birds chirping as they returned to their favoured trees, and our conversation was more jovial. It seemed that maybe I had been too quick to judge. Wau hadn't lost its beauty, it just took me some time to find it.

What it means to be human

As the week in Wau was coming to an end and the ten-day trip through South Sudan nearly over, I began to look back over the journey. Mundri reminded me of the war's impact on people's ability to recover both psychologically from trauma as well as from the physical devastation. Abdi and Sapan were victims of the long war even if they hadn't fought in it; lacking the training and experience they were unable to take the next step to build their own future. As the war wound down and peace found its footing, the international community moved from emergency relief to transitional programming. Our efforts had focused on rebuilding infrastructure and strengthening human capital. There was no doubt we had done a good job with bricks and mortar projects, but as soon as it began to involve people we struggled. We trained village chiefs on issues surrounding sexual and gender-based violence, but they eventually left office. We tried our hand at microfinance without following through. The seventy-year-old Chief Aliyaza was right when he said that we didn't really help people 'realise their potential'.

It wasn't a lack of ideas or courage that had led to failure. Rather, it seems that unrealistic goals meant we were doomed to fail from the start. Money is tendered competitively in a way that encourages hollow promises and wishful thinking. I contributed to this by writing proposals knowing them to be unlikely to succeed under the contractual constraints because I knew that well-grounded ideas and realistic schedules were unlikely to win any funding.

In Wau the problem was different. Our emergency response saved lives, but those same people who we helped through their moment of need were now left languishing without services, ownership of the land they were living on, or jobs. While the solution must begin with the people themselves, their disconnect with the new government is a failure of the international community. Through my trip in South Sudan it became clear that much was being spent on building a state that manages money to deliver services. However, little was being done to build the people's ability to demand representation from that state and to insist on accountability around spending. The people of the Eastern Bank have every right to complain. Since the war ended, the international community has done little but strengthen the hand of the government while weakening the power of the people.

Abdulrahman was right when he spoke of the importance of nurturing a civil society over years and even decades. Without a robust civil society to hold the government to account or to represent the needs of the people or to rally against ineffective and overpaid Western specialists, the system will only serve to entrench power amongst a few.

It seems that at least the international community had done one thing right. The Women's Development Group had been supported by various international donors for over a decade, finally allowing them to find their place in civil society and to play a role in it by, for instance, observing the elections. It may seem a small step but 192 women trained and empowered to adjudicate free and fair elections creates a self-belief and an agency in the women that will remain long after the spotlight on South Sudan has shifted.

One final meeting was on my schedule. While my hope was to see Sister Sarah and to talk to her about Wau since the days of Marco Garang, I learned that she had moved on, to where I wasn't sure. Instead, I arranged to meet with a colleague of hers, Father Martin, also from the Camboni Missionaries of the Catholic Church.

Charles and I headed to the railway station where through the war years the Murahalleen, an Arabic name meaning 'travellers', would shelter. These were the slavers, those who I had watched bring back a dozen slaves bound and tied into Wau all those years ago. I had never visited this area of Wau as when I lived here it was too dangerous, but I had come face to face with the slavers on numerous occasions. They were warriors whose fearsome reputation was, if anything, understated. I was told that they rode into battle on horseback, their dishdasha streaming in the air behind them, turbans tightly wound on their heads and one or even two AK-47s firing into a hapless village or against SPLA fighters. When they came back from one such raid, I had an opportunity to see them up close. The offices of a French NGO I was visiting, Action Contre la Faim, lay directly along their path from the rural areas to the railway station. Not satisfied with the day's raid of about forty cattle, they encircled the compound firing their weapons into the outside wall and in the air. We were on the floor in what we guessed to be the safest room for about twenty minutes, waiting for them to get bored before leaving us alone. Eventually they left, but the next day one of the aid workers stranded in the office with me was evacuated; she couldn't deal with the stress.

It wasn't just the surrounding villagers that feared them but locals in the market place and even officials. A common practice among these tribes was to have small passages of the Koran written onto parchment and then implanted under the skin. It was believed that these charms provided protection against the blade and the bullet. Many people I had met and respected swore to having seeing it work with their own eyes.

Today, though, the area was residential. Father Martin's house had been returned to the Roman Catholic Church after decades of use by the military and their minions. We were welcomed by an aid and guided to a bare earth courtyard where a few flimsy chairs were hastily brought together.

We had first met Father Martin, a tall white-haired Spaniard, a few days earlier when Charles had accompanied me to his church grounds. As I explained my interest in Wau and the reason for visiting, the elderly Father dressed in casual Western clothes responded apologetically by saying, 'I'm not really sure I'll be of much use to you. I'm only new to Wau.'

'How long have you been here?' I asked, a little disappointed as I was hoping to catch someone with a broad perspective on what has been happening over the past few years.

'In Wau? Only eleven years,' he said without a hint of humour.

Father Martin first arrived in Sudan in 1971, though he had spent most of his time in the north, only moving to the south in 1998. When he was leaving the seminary ready to undertake his first posting for God, he was asked to list the top three countries he preferred to be posted to. 'Sudan, Sudan, Sudan,' was his reply.

'When I arrived to Wau it was difficult to find food,' he began to explain after I'd asked him about his memories of coming here. 'Schools didn't have teachers. Sometimes the students would lead the class. In one case I remember the school principal left to get a job as a watchman with an NGO.'

Even though I had come a few years later I remember the situation well enough. Father Martin wasn't exaggerating. I was surprised we'd never crossed paths, but apart from Sister Sarah I had rarely mixed with the missionaries, naively believing their work to be contrary to the secular efforts of the aid industry.

Father Martin continued. 'During the war people were just happy to survive. Wau was like a prison. There was no freedom with a curfew at seven pm and we required a travel permit to move around, but now it has changed.'

'How has it changed?' I asked.

'There is peace. But new problems have come with it: street children, prostitution, and drunkenness. Drinking is a big problem. I sometimes go to meetings in the afternoon and all of the people are already drunk.'

The war and subsequent peace had created broken families, joblessness, disillusionment, anger, and resentment. It was a volatile mix that was palpable, not helped by the large number of foreigners controlling most of the business.

'What are your activities? Is the Church doing something about these new problems?' Charles, who had been listening with reverence, chipped in.

'The Church is teaching against corruption, but the only solution is a strong civil society. We can train people to be the best ministers or professors, but they don't understand what it means to be a citizen.'

With his mission to evangelise and spread the word of Jesus Christ, I had assumed the Father's perspective on the challenges facing South Sudan and his potential solutions would be very different to mine. Yet the ideas were the same—the importance of the community being able to stand up and project its voice.

'It's not enough to teach subjects. We need to teach what it means to be a human being. God gave us a chance to help ourselves and our brothers. The best way to create a nation is to make sure that everyone has a role to play in society.'

This seemed easier said than done, as each village, tribe, community, or individual is different and what works with one doesn't with another. But having people like Father Martin living amongst the community year after year, understanding the hopes and aspirations, challenges and setbacks of the people without offering pre-packaged solutions is essential to success.

'I have a story for you,' he said, as if he was my grandfather passing on a family tale. 'A 4x4 with three Dinka soldiers hit a church car from behind as it was slowing down to turn. The traffic police came to the accident and I was also called to come. The officer was a Dinka; upon looking at the situation he decided that the church would have to pay for the repairs of both vehicles. I asked who was at fault according to the law, but he wouldn't answer. His relations and loyalty were more important than rules and the law. Will writing more laws change this situation? I don't think so. We need to work with society to change and this takes time.'

A faltering façade

Two months after I left, the people of South Sudan woke to the day they had been dreaming of for decades, even generations. People queued peacefully outside village polling stations, along main streets, and in schools and health centres. They were there to play their role as citizens in this newly established democracy by voicing their opinion on the direction of their future. The television cameras were there alongside print journalists from around the world to record the moment for perpetuity. Democracy had reached the heart of Africa.

As I watched the week of voting unfold, I wondered what democracy meant to the people I had met. The government will now be closer to the people and certainly, for the first time in decades, of the people, but would it be for the people? The international community worked hard to build its framework by establishing a constitution, passing laws and seating a parliament, but what about the people? No one had worked with Chief Angelo to help him and his 70,000 displaced, soon to be destitute, men, women and children learn how to work within this new system of government to secure their property rights. Neither the New Sudan Women's Federation nor the Mundri Youth Development Association knew what role they could play in the long march to a democracy that must go beyond holding a few ballots. The only community organisation that seemed to have flourished and could fit the bill as a voice of the people—the Women's Development group—took ten years to nurture. Was it just that I had visited the wrong places at the wrong time to come to the conclusion that civil society had been forgotten? To check I went to the list of projects supported through the Multi-Donor Trust Fund for South Sudan into which international donors pooled their resources or coordinated their activities. A total of 593 million dollars had been pledged by countries around the world to support the development of the new country. Of that amount, not a cent was specifically allocated to strengthening the people's ability to understand their roles and responsibilities in a democratic state.

So while money was allocated to bolstering the police forces (such as those who ruled against Father Martin in the traffic violation), nothing was being spent on informing the people of their rights or creating an avenue of recourse when tribal relations trumped the rule of law. There are plans to establish a government town planning and land administration unit, but even if this eventually happens, it's unlikely to help Chief Angelo protect his people's land against government appropriation as it will be controlled by the same government officials. Funds have been allocated to pay for a bureaucracy to support an anti-corruption unit, yet there is no mention of efforts to train and support investigative journalists, anti-corruption NGOs, and the legal fraternity that together form the bulwark against corruption. The infrastructure of a democratic government was being established, but the only people who might know how to use it would be government officials.

Not surprisingly then, it didn't take long for the democratic façade to falter. In 2013 conflict broke out between the supporters of the President, Salva Kiir, and his Vice President, Riek Machar. The power struggle spiralled into an ethnic battle between the Dinka and Nuer tribes with atrocities committed against civilians. The conflict continues to rage across the young country, with an estimated 300,000 deaths and millions displaced.

Even if development resources are distributed more evenly between strengthening the government and helping the people hold them accountable, who would deliver this aid? The aid community has proven itself competent in completing the easiest elements of rebuilding countries. They hire specialists to draw up appropriate legislation, contract construction companies to build offices or hire experts to organise the ever popular but much abused study tours. The much more difficult part, but one that's largely ignored, is to work with the society to change society. Is the aid industry ready for this challenge? With funding that is largely short term and driven by political expectations, can we support slow, complex and often incomprehensible (to us) grassroots efforts to change society?

And even if we could, who would spend the years or decades working with the people as Dorothy Apples did or Father Martin is still doing? There is a shortage of competent aid workers willing to rough it alongside the people. As Peter and Matthew said, the problem is the people—the aid workers. It's rare to see among the aid community a commitment to a country such as that exhibited by Father Martin. Apart from five years working on Iraq my attention to a country and its people has been as fleeting as most others.

The consequence is that we deliver cookie-cutter solutions picked up from the last posting on the other side of the world as a substitute for the much more difficult process of working with the people to develop a context-specific approach. Locally geared aid where people live within and amongst the community, learn about their values and culture, and then support the people in their chosen direction, such as what Charles spoke of, is rarely seen. I have had expatriates complain because they don't have twenty-four-hour electricity or internet at home, that the beds are not comfortable enough or that fans are no substitute for air conditioners. On the one hand it shouldn't be a surprise; what used to be a few good souls sent abroad with a handshake and a handful of cash has become an industry requiring master's degrees and business acumen to manage tens or hundreds of millions of dollars. But along this inescapable process of professionalisation, our focus on the end goal has been lost. As Chief Aliyaza said, the key is 'realising people's potential,' and that takes time and patience. It takes a very different character than a corporate MBA looking to bring business practices to the aid industry or the military's can-do attitude. Yet this is who we're hiring, and evidently this is who I was at risk of becoming: someone familiar with the corporate culture but ignorant to the culture on the ground.

General Kilo's contingent assessing the breakdown

The author drinking tea at Sapan's Wakil Allah Guest House

The author with Susan

Lucia making bread

A broken clothes washing point in Eastern Bank Camp

Chief Angelo Uraya Dut on the left, Charles in centre

The Women's Development Group team

PART TWO
Iraq

A beard for every situation

Baghdad in April is one of the more pleasant places in the Middle East. The mornings have a zesty chill to them, but the day quickly warms. The skies in April are an endless deep blue and cloudless, a perfect backdrop for the many birds that take centre stage in the mornings. The calls of the muezzin summoning the faithful to prayer add a soothing, hypnotic score. Under other circumstances this city would be one of the finest travel destinations in the world, steeped in history, culture, and religious significance. In April 2004, however, the endless blue sky was stained by streaks of camouflage green as military helicopters moved restlessly. Not for the first or last time the preparations for battle and the regular deep thuds of mortars and car bombs destroyed any sense of tranquillity.

And now that general lack of tranquillity had descended into outright dread. It was midnight and Firas Shaheed, the senior Iraqi staff member in Najaf, was on the phone. 'Fadi has been taken from his house.'

It took a while for Firas to go through the details of the kidnapping: at eleven pm two pickups carrying eighteen or nineteen men came to our two houses in the Teachers' Quarter of Najaf. Heavily armed with AK-47s and RPGs, they swiftly subdued the guard positioned in the street, preventing him from setting into motion our elaborate security warning system—a whistle. The men banged on the outside gate of the house and demanded the doors be opened, claiming to be from the religious courts. Once inside it was a quick and easy process of finding 'incriminating' evidence—including a bottle of vinegar that they thought was alcohol and a Spanish DVD that apparently had an indecent cover—before grabbing the foreigner. The men pushed Fadi down the stairs, grabbed his Canadian passport, and forced him into our parked car, leaving the guard to find Firas and tell him what had happened.

Fadi had only joined us a month earlier, tasked with leading efforts to help children overcome the traumas of war. Some weeks earlier, not knowing that the country was about to collapse into mayhem, I had decided not to evacuate Fadi along with the other expatriates as he was of Syrian heritage, spoke Arabic, and generally fit into the Najafi scene. So Fadi remained behind as the only expatriate from mid-March until early April, when I was supposed to join him. The day before he was kidnapped, as the security situation had deteriorated precipitously, I had spoken with Fadi and told him to move to a safe house rather than risk leaving the city and running the dangerous gauntlet of checkpoints manned by Muqtadr al-Sadr's powerful Mehdi Army, along with other threats such as opportunistic criminals and various insurgent groups. For some reason that I didn't know at that stage, he had ignored my instructions to go to the safe house, a location I had prearranged months earlier to ensure expatriates had somewhere to lie low.

My regular morning ritual became eating porridge with Norman, our Scottish security officer and former SAS bomb disposal specialist, while watching the growing tally of Westerners who'd been kidnapped. One Italian told his captors before he was beheaded, 'I will show you how an Italian dies.' I couldn't imagine Fadi saying the same. He was a gentle social worker who found comfort in quietly helping people. He wasn't prone to heroic statements or actions.

Restricted for security reasons to our house and to our office across the street we set up a crisis management team, sat close to the phones and settled in for the known knowns, the unknown knowns and the unknown unknowns, to paraphrase the then US Secretary of Defence Donald Rumsfeld. As we had the contacts, personnel and relationships in Najaf, it was agreed with the Baghdad based Canadian government liaison, the headquarters of our employers, the International Rescue Committee (IRC), and the Coalition Provisional Authority (CPA) that we'd be the focal point of the effort.

Our office in Baghdad, a single-storey house with a well-kept lawn in a walled courtyard, was buzzing with activity. Between all the guards we had one lone AK-47, which was pitiful compared with the heat packed by other families on our street. At both ends of the street our neighbours were heavily armed and had proven trusted companions when previous threats had emerged. As the number of attacks against other organisations in Baghdad rose we later added a second semi-automatic weapon, although this was still less weaponry than could be found at most Iraqi weddings. We weren't so naïve as to believe that two weapons would protect us against attack, but NGO protocols prevented us from taking a heavily fortified approach to security, so our strategy in case of an assault—quite a simple one actually—was to run, and we practised evacuations to make sure we were prepared. Otherwise our hope lay in the anonymity that a large city such as Baghdad affords, unlike in Najaf where there were only two foreign organisations with expatriates in the whole city.

Feeling responsible for the kidnapping, Firas sprang to action by mobilising his relatives. The Shaheed family has a number of well-respected religious scholars, including Firas' father and grandfather. Both men wear the black turban signifying a scholar of the Koran with direct lineage from the Prophet Muhammad. They also both grow their beards long. In Najaf, the longer a religious scholar's beard the more respected and esteemed he is. So, when the three generations of Shaheeds, including the grandfather, a man of over eighty years of age with a beard to his chest, went to visit the young Muqtadr seeking help, it was a gesture full of meaning—elderly and respected religious scholars reaching out to the young upstart. The grandfather's presence made us hopeful of our pleas being heard. As it turned out, grandfather Firas' beard was clearly not as long as the situation required, and the visit proved fruitless. Not deterred the family continued their efforts over the coming days by reaching out to childhood friends and relatives, in the process, exposing themselves as sympathisers of the Americans and potentially risking their lives in an effort to help a stranger. I was staggered by the courage and moral fortitude required to take such action.

As the city that was once the epicentre of civilisation devolved back to primal law with gunmen roaming the streets hunting Westerners, I noticed myself becoming angry and disappointed. Our entire operation, programs that had reached so many people in need, were now at risk because my staff forgot that they were in the middle of a war zone or thought they knew better. Fadi was not the only kidnapping victim; two other Iraqi staff had also been kidnapped separately while driving past Muqtadr al-Sadr's mosque and filming it.

Yet, through the course of attempting to free Fadi I was also heartened. We discovered the courage and compassion of our staff and the wider community as well as some less heartening information about some murky connections. One of our drivers was secretly a member of the Mehdi Army, but with a growing sympathy for IRC via the friendships he had fostered. Upon hearing of Fadi's kidnapping he immediately drew on his contacts and went to the senior leadership asking for support. He was promised that Fadi would be released—a promise that indicated to us who was holding him. Our hopes rose. Shortly after, he was bluntly told that the Mehdi Army did not have Fadi. Our hopes were dashed. The bearded trio visited the head of al-Sadr's religious court, Sheikh Jabr, explaining the situation and asking for help. They were told he would call them back later that evening after prayers. Our hopes rose. He didn't call. They were dashed. We had tribal chiefs working on our behalf. One was given assurances that he would be released the next day. Our hopes were raised. He never was. Our hopes were dashed. And so it continued.

We were still in the dark as to who had Fadi and for what reason. Was it money? Political leverage? Local dispute? Then on the third day, I was called to the television where several of the guards were standing around intently watching an Iranian news program. There was some footage of two haggard men, dressed in flowing dishdasha, the long robes worn by men in the Middle East, kneeling on a concrete floor. Each man made a short speech. They introduced themselves as Nabil George Yaakob Razuq and Ahmed Yassin Tikati. Their captors, faces covered, stood ominously to each side. The gun-wielding characters called themselves Ansar Al-Din, perhaps a reference to the military units that fought alongside Salah al-Din when he drove the Crusaders out of the Levant in the twelfth century.

Both captors admitted on camera, though clearly under coercion, that they were Israeli spies. It was a hung jury among our guards whether the latter, the poor Mr Tikati, was our Fadi. They didn't show a close-up, the footage wasn't clear and the lighting cast shadows across the haggard faces, making it hard to identify the captives. My initial feeling was driven by hope. The face looked worn, too old for Fadi's thirty-three years. Not long after, while we were still trying to agree on who Mr Tikati was, the scrolling ticker at the bottom of the screen read in Farsi that a Syrian Canadian had been captured as a spy working for an organisation called IRC. Not only were the Iranians reporting that he was a spy but shortly after Yasser Arafat became involved. The former Palestinian leader signed a letter calling for the release of the two 'Palestinians', wrongly referring to Ahmed Yassin Tikati, aka Fadi Fadel, as a resident of East Jerusalem! These misrepresentations badly damaged our efforts to convince the domestic and international media of his Canadian nationality and Syrian heritage, also giving the dangerous impression that we were part of an Israeli cover-up.

***

Iraq circa 2004

In late March 2004 a series of incidents began to unfold in Iraq that would significantly change how humanitarian organisations operated. The first spark flared on 28 March when US troops closed the offices of a newspaper run by the firebrand cleric and heir to a respected religious name, Muqtadr al-Sadr. By the end of the day thousands of Shia were protesting what they saw as an undemocratic and hypocritical move.

A few days later, several hundred kilometres away in the Sunni city of Falluja, four foreign security contractors returning from a meeting in the governor's building were ambushed in the streets of the so-called 'City of Mosques'. Beaten and set alight by the mob, their charred bodies were paraded through the city and eventually two were strung from a bridge. The world was shocked by this brazen and barbaric act. Television footage showed bystanders rushing to the scene, but rather than aiding the men, they kicked and spat on the bodies. Pressure was mounting on the US to do something.

Following the closure of the newspaper on 3 April, a close deputy to al-Sadr, Mustafa al-Yacoubi, was arrested by the Americans for complicity in the murder of al-Khoei, a senior and respected moderate Ayatollah. In response al-Sadr's followers led protests throughout the South. In Najaf, a city eighty kilometres south of Baghdad, twenty Iraqis and four Salvadorian soldiers were killed, and more than two hundred people were injured in the subsequent clashes.

Over the next two days Sadr was calling on his followers to 'terrorise the enemy' as US forces surrounded Falluja prepared to attack and Sunni religious leaders were threatening

Holy War. It was a conflagration that threatened to tear the country and the Middle East apart.

This wasn't just a deterioration of the security situation, something that generations of aid workers had faced before. It signalled a shift in how those with the means and intent to kill saw foreign aid workers. The US had become involved in the local politics and by extension this made all Westerners proxies to one side or another, be it in localised turf battles or the wider cultural wars that were pushing aside tradition in favour of new ideas and power structures.

* * *

By 14 April, eight days into the saga, we were beginning to fear that it would not be hours or days but weeks and perhaps months before Fadi was freed, if at all. We tried to keep the worst out of our minds. It was around this time that I was briefed by headquarters on information on Fadi's past that was becoming public. The details were only sketchy but it appeared that Fadi had lived and worked on the streets of Montreal to survive after a falling out with his family who didn't react well to learning that he was gay. I later read that his experiences living on the streets for two years were what led him to social work as he saw the poverty and destitution first hand. He wanted to help others, he had told interviewers, even though he was the one in need of support. Eventually he went to university and started working on issues such as child trafficking and sexual exploitation of minors, before joining us in Iraq.

Baghdad that April wasn't the place where I expected guests to drop by, and certainly not people who were from out of town. Headquarters had arranged for a kidnap and ransom specialist to give advice and support. I didn't expect that he'd physically come knocking on our door. But one day, from the empty streets of Baghdad, a tall Englishman named Les Edwards arrived at our doorstep. With his public school accent and pressed shirts it felt surreal, verging on comic considering the circumstances. I sat with him to go through what had happened as well as to cover off on our future plans. We talked about other cases and how they had worked out. He stayed a few hours and then flew out to Amman where he continued to provide ongoing support.

One of the ideas that sprung from my discussions with Les was to write a letter directly to al-Sadr. The kidnapping was reported as having being led by Ansar al Din. Publicly they had no association with al-Sadr's Mehdi Army, although privately we were very aware of a close relationship, if not actual overlap, between the two. So I drafted a letter calling for help to negotiate with Ansar al Din. We heaped praise on Sadr's father and his grandfather and the long tradition of his family; and on his wisdom and standing in society. Our hope was to encourage al-Sadr to grab this opportunity to appear as the benevolent and successful negotiator, rather than be found and accused subsequently of being responsible for the kidnapping. We printed several of these letters and addressed them to various representatives of al-Sadr in the hope that at least one would get to him.

The ordeal came to an abrupt end ten days after it had started. I took a call late in the evening from headquarters informing me that a Reuter's journalist had contacted them about a press conference al-Sadr's office had organised to announce their successful intervention in the release of Fadi Fadel. He wanted to help; he offered to give Fadi his satellite phone so he could speak with someone. We decided that I would be the point of contact, so I waited for the call. Within half an hour Fadi was on the other line, having just been released and about to enter the press conference. He only had a few minutes. The first words that he said to me were, 'Denis, I promise I'll always listen to your advice in the future. I have been thinking about it every day.' I didn't need the apology, I just wanted to get him out, and despite being released from the kidnappers we still needed to get him to Baghdad.

None of us listened to the press conference. Instead, we started planning the logistics of getting Fadi out. This was not going to be an easy task as battles still raged in the city and around the country, including in the areas between Najaf and Baghdad. We decided against moving him to a nearby US Marines' base as it would have confirmed the perception that foreign organisations were a front for the military, and those Iraqis who had helped him would be at great risk because they would then be perceived to be American spies. Taking him to the Coalition Provisional Authority (CPA) compound was out of the question as it was still under siege. The plan we adopted was to drive Fadi to Baghdad's airport and fly him out of the country as soon as possible. It was too late that night for any road movement, so he'd have to spend one more night in Najaf, which must have been hell for him but at least he would enjoy his first night of being free.

The press conference was held near the religious court. Our team, lying low among the crowd, waited for the conference to end and then hustled Fadi away to the home of the family of one of our guards. The blow-back for this well-known family could have been enormous as it meant potentially being targeted as collaborators. I was once again overwhelmed by the risks our staff were willing to take for Fadi's sake. There was still a long road ahead of us, so we decided to get to bed early that night, though not before Norman and I indulged in a celebratory bottle of beer.

The next morning we sent two powerful 7 Series BMWs from Baghdad with our most experienced drivers behind the wheel. They were to meet the car coming from Najaf halfway on the bridge over the river Euphrates just north of Babylon. Some of our staff proposed putting their family members, women and children, in the car to give the perception of a family travelling to Baghdad. I overruled those offers and instead asked for volunteers. Three male staff members put their hands up, leaving Najaf as scheduled in the morning. Fadi was now on the final stretch home, but the risks were still high. Travellers in Baghdad were under constant threat with random shootings, car bombs, and vehicle hijackings a common occurrence.

While Fadi was being driven to Baghdad I also got into a car and headed for the airport to meet the Jordanian doctor waiting to assess Fadi's health and his ability to fly. Once there I waited together with the Canadian liaison, a gaggle of spooks, and a few others who seemed to have an interest in the proceedings but weren't ready to identify themselves.

An hour or so later Fadi reached the safety of the airport without incident. We embraced and had a few laughs. It was good to see him healthy and in high spirits and to know that, at least in our case, the story ended well. Fadi returned to Canada, shaken but in one piece. The remaining staff largely slid back into the shadows of Najaf society. I heard of only one who apparently suffered retributions, a bashing by unknown assailants for his association with the effort to release Fadi. Muqtadr got recognition as a humanitarian, albeit short lived and wholly unjustified. Importantly for me, we weren't forced to shut down our operations. It was a few more months before that instruction came through.

Managing a kidnapping case in a war zone wasn't the skill set I thought I'd need when I left the sedate and structured profession of engineering. But whether it was the adrenalin or the constant reminder of the fickleness of life I felt more alive than ever during this time. That it involved a friend of mine and knowing that I was ultimately responsible for his situation by not pulling him out of Najaf along with the other expatriates made it very real. I also felt strangely grateful for the chance to see the dark underbelly of the political-criminal kidnapping endeavour.

* * *

The Kidnapping Business Model

Since the 2004 kidnapping of Fadi there has been a lot of debate about civilian presence in war zones and whether they do more harm than good by offering militants a potential source of income. A 2015 Congressional Research Service report has compiled information on revenue earned from kidnappings by various terrorist groups. According to the report, Islamic State collected $35-45 million in ransom fees in 2014, al-Qaeda in the Arabian Peninsula an estimated $20 million in ransom between 2011 and 2013, and al-Qaeda in the Islamic Maghreb an estimated $75 million since 2010. While the majority of this income is derived from ransoms paid for kidnapped locals, some is derived from the release of captured Western journalists and aid workers.

Fundamentalist Islamic groups such as Islamic State and al-Qaeda differ in their views on this matter. Al-Qaeda has taken a more nuanced approach to the kidnapping of Western aid workers than Islamic State. According to reports compiled by the Brookings Institute, on at least two occasions, senior leaders of the al-Qaeda linked Syrian group, Jabhat al-Nusra, implored Islamic State to release Western aid workers on the basis that kidnapping and executing them was 'wrong under Islamic law' and 'counter-productive'.

The solution isn't as simple as withdrawing civilian personnel and leaving the military to do the work as both sides acknowledge. The dispute is over the balance between military and civilian responsibilities and approaches. According to a report prepared by Fourth Freedom Forum and the Kroc Institute at the University of Notre Dame, 'Counterterrorism experts traditionally argued that the struggle against terrorist insurgency is eighty per cent non-military. A senior Pentagon advisor has stated more recently that the struggle is one hundred per cent non-military.'

The dominant strategy in Iraq and Afghanistan of high security walls and impenetrable compounds has served international workers well, but has stymied their ability to achieve their goals. A different model needs to be sought, one in which risks are minimised while development outcomes remain in view. Such an approach requires an enhanced focus on local capacity and leadership. This may mean less transparency and a compromise on results in the short term but better outcomes in the long term.

In those circumstances, where expatriates are necessary and the security situation is precarious, the risk should only be taken if the organisation is deeply entrenched in the community. If we hadn't had the extensive relationships within Najaf I suspect that Fadi's release may not have occurred. For agencies that have operated successfully with years or decades of positive relationships, then the risks can be greatly minimised, but this takes a long-term commitment, vision and adherence to a strategy that doesn't simply prioritise short-term outcomes.

Plotting an assassination

As I was completing my return to Najaf, the US had completed its withdrawal of combat forces with the last departing just weeks earlier, leaving behind only advisors and trainers. Indiscriminate attacks still continued, though not as intense as in previous years. As I prepared for my trip from Amman, I was told that the situation was tense.

The city of Najaf, with a population of less than a million people, is perched between the Euphrates and the prosaically named Sea of Najaf, a desert expanse reaching all the way to Saudi Arabia. Some locals profess with hand on heart that the desert was underwater during the great flood after which Noah's Ark came to rest in the nearby town of Kufa. Today, all that remains of where their ancestors may have once stood dipping their toes in the gentle waves lapping against the foreshore are steep cliffs, at the bottom of which boiler makers, metal fabricators, and other soot-covered professionals ply their trade. Standing by the cliff's edge looking down, I was reminded of the Leprosy pits in Ben Hur.

I was nervous about flying into a war zone without any organisational support, but having an extended network of friends in Najaf comforted me when I contemplated the possibilities of something going wrong. With criminal gangs, militants and militias well established in this particular corner of Iraq and anti-Western sentiment strong, it was a very real threat. Regardless of whether visiting for a few days or establishing a new aid operation, perceptions of who you are and what your intentions are matter. Not to the criminal gangs or extremists, but to influential leaders, staff, their neighbours and friends—people who are best placed to protect you. This was a lesson that a leading ayatollah taught me not long after my first arrival in Iraq.

* * *

Within months after the 2003 invasion of Iraq, the security situation began to deteriorate. Alongside the vague outline of an emerging insurgency was the clearly defined, full-fledged power struggle between the ayatollahs living in Najaf. The metaphorical first shot came in early April with the knifing of the presumed leader of the moderate faction within the Shia religious hierarchy, Ayatollah Abdul Majid al Khoei. A few months later on 29 August I was shaken by a car bomb three kilometres away at the Imam Ali Shrine. The explosion turned out to be one of the deadliest in Iraq, killing one hundred and twenty-five people including Ayatollah Mohammed Baqir al Hakim, another leading cleric. It was time for the ayatollahs to go into hiding, and many did by either fleeing to Iran or bunkering down under heavy layers of security.

Being an unregulated religious space, Shia Islam pits ayatollah against ayatollah in a rivalry for the hearts, minds and pay cheques of believers. There isn't a single unified hierarchy and this creates competition, which is starkly manifested in Najaf and Karbala where many religious leaders and scholars reside. Under better circumstances this competition would be reputational—whose scholarship was most respected, whose piety most admired, whose rulings most sought after. In turn the faithful who choose to follow an Ayatollah would fulfil their religious obligations of zakat—contributing a portion of their income and assets for humanitarian purposes, with an additional contribution required of Shia Muslims called *khums*—through an ayatollah's personal charity. Together this creates a substantial redistribution of wealth from the well-off to the poor, in effect a Muslim tax and welfare system. The funds are used to support couples about to marry, families up against hard times, even providing money to fund funerals. In addition, the funds are sometimes used in a way more familiar to Western charities such as distributing food and clothes, providing medical care, and supporting the disabled and incapacitated. This not only makes religious leaders in Shia Islam morally influential with broad mass appeal but considerable actors in the humanitarian and social services space. Unfortunately, the rivalry between clerics was having much broader ramifications for everyone involved.

As my own security and that of our staff and projects was tied to our relations with the community and its religious leaders, I continued to visit the various clerics who decided to remain behind. In a decision that I was to rue a few months later when we suspected his people were behind Fadi's kidnapping, I had an appointment to meet Muqtadr al Sadr, the son of a grand ayatollah and soon to be thorn in the American side. Blissfully unaware of how our paths were to cross again and the role he was to play in the future of Iraq, I did not meet with him on that occasion due to a scheduling conflict. Three days after my visit to another cleric, Ayatollah Muhammad Said al-Hakim, a bomb exploded in front of his offices, killing his guard and injuring several others. But of all the ayatollahs I had the opportunity to visit, my time with Grand Ayatollah Sheikh Bashir was one of the most illuminating as well as nerve-wracking.

Though he first joined us as a driver after leaving the teaching profession that was paying five dollars a month in the dying days of Saddam's regime, by late 2003 Firas held the position of Operations Manager for the IRC Najaf office. Not only did his demeanour exude piety, but according to his tribe's traditions he is a direct descendant of Prophet Mohammad through Imam Hussein, son of Imam Ali who was the cousin of the Prophet and husband to his daughter. As Firas was the son and grandson of respected clerics, he became my go-between when organising meetings with religious figures. He was well connected and well versed in the protocols and politics of the clerics and ayatollahs of Najaf.

One October evening together with Firas and his long-time friend and IRC colleague Haider, I got into a car and headed downtown to meet with the Grand Ayatollah Sheikh Bashir. The Ayatollah's offices can be found in the old quarter of Najaf, a stone's throw (or a rifle shot) away from other competing clerics vying to remain within hearing distance of the muezzin's call to the faithful, exhorting them to prayer from a minaret high above the Shrine of Imam Ali. That evening the drive to the old town took us through narrow thoroughfares faintly lit by street lamps striking sand still in the air from a late summer sandstorm. Dilapidated two- and three-storey houses shakily crowded over the streets in a show of either godly humility or human neglect. Men sauntered home from mosques in their dishdasha, while the women in their head to toe black abayas scurried out of sight.

We came to a road block, one more reminder of the pre-eminence of the affairs of man in this avowedly holy city. A few men, scattered amongst the shadows, pointed their Kalashnikovs at us while another stood in the headlights with arm raised, challenging our arrival. After introducing ourselves as staff members of the IRC, we were led by a guard to a metal door, which he entered to check our appointment. Verified as scheduled guests we were welcomed inside, searched for weapons, shown where we could leave our shoes, and then led into a small windowless room with a worn brown carpet. The interior of the Ayatollah's residence was surprising and impressively modest for a leader of such status. Furniture was sparse, limited to a small wooden cabinet serving as a bookcase that would be lucky to have raised a few dollars at a junkyard sale. We waited, accompanied by the office manager and, a little while later Ayatollah Bashir's son.

For several minutes we engaged in standard small talk—they asked my first impressions of Iraq, I asked them their thoughts on the war, we each answered with what we assumed the other wanted to hear. Then the Ayatollah entered. He was, in appearance, carved from the same stone as leaders of a bygone era, from a time when great men exuded an intoxicating aura of authority and wisdom. But in today's world of slick haircuts and Hollywood smiles the close-up matters—and in this case it wasn't pretty. With a long unkempt salt-and-pepper beard, rolls of fat, and skin the texture of a worn prayer rug, the Ayatollah was a study in the rejection of modernism. He wore a white turban suggesting that his ancestors were not from the Prophet's blood line. A black robe covered his white dishdasha and a pair of thick, black-rimmed glasses was firmly planted on his nose.

We sat on the cushions and carpet. With some Ayatollahs I would kneel and kiss their hands, inches above the ground, as a sign of respect. For some reason it didn't seem appropriate that I would make the gesture, nor did he reach out expecting it. Was this a reflection of his disposition? I wasn't sure, so I prepared for the standard introduction.

Instead, the Ayatollah began by telling Firas, who subsequently translated for me, that he could not speak English. I understood this and cut in to Firas' translation, 'But as I am visiting Iraq it is I who should apologise that I cannot speak Arabic.'

His expression remained impassive, impenetrable, and continuing to talk in Arabic with Firas he countered, 'But English is an important language, the most important for all people in the world. I would like to have learned it, but in my role as the leader of all Shia people I must study many other things.'

I continued with flattery, 'Those things that you study, to help you as a leader, are more important than English.' I hoped that this exchange would win him over. This was unlike other meetings with religious leaders, during which we discussed Western academic accounts of the schism between Shia and Sunni Islam in the seventh century or the finer points of Imam Ali's betrayal. The Ayatollah asked if he could speak frankly to me, to which I replied that I would welcome such a conversation.

'What are your ties to the CIA?' he demanded, explaining that all Western organisations have links to the CIA. Before I could reply, the Ayatollah accused me of assessing the layout and security within his compound with an eye to plotting an assassination. This was not a good beginning. Firas didn't want to translate it initially, but the Ayatollah gestured quite forcefully that he must. I replied carefully, not wanting to appear dismissive, trying to find the right balance between his suspicions and reality. 'Maybe at a higher level it is possible that organisations do have connections with the CIA, but on the ground, those of us who implement the projects don't have any connections. We operate independently.'

Firas was squirming at this point, reluctant to translate every word. Around this point in the conversation, I learned later, the Ayotallah also berated Firas for shaving off his beard. Being a direct descendent of the Prophet, and his father and grandfather well known and well regarded religious scholars, in the eyes of the Ayatollah, Firas should have respected his religion by letting it grow. Instead Firas chose to go with the more common seven-day growth, neatly trimmed in length and cut sharply around the edges. I glanced at him from the corner of my eye, wondering if he was ruing the day he gave up his teaching position to work alongside an alleged spy while being berated by an ayatollah for disrespecting his own religion. Usually he was very good at using humour to defuse a tense situation, a valuable trait under Saddam's regime, I imagined. But now there was no smile, no wry remark or witty comment. He was clearly unnerved by the circumstances. Haider similarly remained silent, sitting cross-legged and inscrutable. Like Firas, Haider had been trained as a teacher, but the similarities ended there. Haider was wiry thin, clean shaven, and often played second fiddle to Firas' more exuberant personality. Even so, his silence now seemed out of place.

The Ayatollah continued, wondering how it was that I could claim to be independent as an Australian when my country invaded Iraq. His logic was simple: 'Your government sent you here!'

I was kneeling, bent over lower than usual, not sure whether out of humility or fear. I didn't really understand the Ayatollah's politics. He was berating Australia for helping to get rid of Saddam, even though the dictator was responsible for oppressing the Shia and killing tens if not hundreds of thousands. I didn't dare ask, and ultimately his politics weren't my business. Instead, I explained that the Australian government didn't know I was there, that my being in Iraq was a consequence of my chosen profession—not my nationality. The Ayatollah continued with increasingly serious gestures, demanding to know what we did and who funded us. I tried to avoid answering the latter by dragging out the answer to the former: 'Among other things, we rehabilitate water treatment plants; provide equipment, training and supplies to health clinics; repair schools; and provide hygiene education to children.'

The Ayatollah cut in with a story about how one organisation, which he could not name because he couldn't read the English, came to distribute clothes, which were colourful, short sleeved, and included things he could not politely describe. Such actions were corrupting young women. 'Are you doing the same?' he asked.

'No,' I replied, using simple English to ensure the message was clear. 'We are not here to change your culture.' At least I wished we weren't. The problem was that the invasion, sold variously as a national security or humanitarian endeavour, had morphed into a rebuilding of Iraqi society. Rewriting the constitution, entrenching gender rights, imposing a liberal market economy, and reworking the social security system—the initial limited endeavour to remove Saddam Hussein had become a remaking of Iraqi society. For Iraqis and the few foreigners such as myself who lived outside of the walled compounds of the Green Zone, it became apparent that this wholesale change was inherent to the effort. Despite isolated attempts to respond to the people's hopes and desires, the juggernaut would recalibrate and continue in its remodelling of Iraq in its own image.

'We are staffed by Iraqis and managed by Iraqis,' I continued.

'Here in Najaf I am the only foreigner in our organisation.' I described our recent planning session, during which the Iraqi staff led in deciding what programs we would implement and how we would allocate funds. 'There are many different organisations...' I began to explain. 'Some take money from the CPA...'

'What is the CPA?'

'Paul Bremer...' I began.

'Paul Bremer is the devil.'

Okay, I remember thinking to myself before collecting my thoughts. I didn't particularly like Bremer either but I was pretty sure that he wasn't the devil. A mix of positive facial expressions and a readiness to blame the translation seemed my best response. Not quite a fool-proof plan, but it had to do.

'So...' taking a deep breath, I began with a very basic overview of the international humanitarian and development industry, '... some organisations take money from the CPA, some have no experience and come here with little idea of what they are doing, some come to spread the word of the Bible, while others are professional independent organisations that work on the basic needs of people. We are non-religious, we are not-for-profit, and all of us came here voluntarily. We are open and transparent and I would like to invite one of your representatives to visit our projects.'

'Who is your funder?' He must have had savvy advisors as he was focused on getting an answer to this question, but at least I had some time to think of a response.

'We have different donors—average people who donate money by, for example, putting money into tin cans at supermarkets. Secondly, we get money from rich people who, when they die, donate their estate...'

'Yes,' he said, 'very much like we do...'

Finally, something in common! I emphasised this point and mentioned it again, hoping that the direction of the conversation would change before I had to explain why we took American government money. I continued, 'We get money from UNICEF...'

Interrupting again, he stated, 'UNICEF is a part of the UN. They are not independent, are they?'

It was a commonly held perception. As a result, months earlier the UN headquarters had been attacked by a massive truck borne bomb that killed the Secretary-General's Special Representative, Sergio Vieira de Mello, along with twenty-one of his staff.

At this stage I decided to just get it over with and plough through. 'We write proposals that we then offer to various donors. We are not contractors; we include the Iraqi staff when we decide what we want to do, and then we offer a proposal to donors to see if they will give us the money for the project.' I watched intently as the translation was delivered. 'One of our donors is OFDA. They are a part of the US government, but,' and I diverted from the intricate details here by simply saying, 'they are the only agency that offers money without political strings attached. OFDA stands for the Office of Foreign Disaster Assistance. They give us money to do as we deem appropriate during an emergency. Other parts of the US government tell organisations what to do; those organisations are contractors. We do not work that way.'

Admittedly, this was an abridged version. A fuller explanation would have noted that although we weren't contracted to implement specific activities, we were obliged to work towards agreed goals that had to align with US policy. In the case of my activities for the IRC, these goals were focused upon internally displaced persons and other humanitarian issues, though there was nuanced disagreement between the donor and the NGO as to who was the most in need. This difference of opinion, though, paled in comparison to the chasm separating Western concepts of need relative to those of Islam. For one thing, there is a focus upon orphans and widows. In the Koran it says, 'They ask you about giving: say, "The charity you give shall go to the parents, the relatives, the orphans, the poor, and the travelling alien."' (2:215). While directives within the hadith emphasise the need of widows: 'One who cares for widows and the poor is like those who fight in the way of Allah or those who spend their days fasting and their nights praying.' Even more problematically for Western aid agencies, many Islamic institutions and groups prioritise helping Muslims over non-Muslims, largely through the rules of who can receive zakat. I decided that evening wasn't the right time to raise these points of contention.

The Ayatollah sat back silently, glaring at me through his thick bifocal glasses. I looked everywhere but in his direction. In fact, he had drawn his conclusions and they were not hostile. He quickly smoothed over the US government funding issue and continued amicably. Politely he suggested that he hoped one day I would become a Muslim.

'I have only been in Iraq for four months,' I told him sincerely, 'and I am learning Arabic. I am learning about Najaf, and about Islam. One day, if my heart takes me, maybe I will follow in the path of Allah.'

That pleased him some more. He nodded ever so slightly, and the tone of the conversation continued to lighten. Fixing his gaze on me even more firmly, the Ayatollah began a parable about Imam Ali. One day Imam Ali came alongside a visiting Christian travelling in the same direction. They decided to walk together as Ali's destination was along the way of the Christian's. As they passed Ali's house the Christian asked why he did not stop. Imam Ali replied that good men should accompany all visitors to ensure their safety and comfort along their path home. I had an image in my mind of hundreds of thousands of American soldiers being accompanied by Saddam's soldiers marching under the Hands of Victory monument. I guess parables are contextual. I didn't know how to interpret this. Did he mean that he would accompany our organisation in its path? I mentioned that many good people of Najaf had welcomed me and accompanied me along my path.

At the end of the nearly two-hour meeting he apologised for being so blunt. The Ayatollah said that it is hard to distinguish a snake from a rope and this I understood. In fact, it was a lesson I had learned repeatedly in Iraq.

'If there is anything that you need, visit me,' he said. 'I will treat you like my own son. I hope to see you again.'

I left wondering how much he knew of what was going on behind the scenes in Iraq. In the years that followed our first meeting with the Ayatollah, I kept in touch through intermediaries. I heard that during Friday prayers he continued to speak kindly of the work we were trying to accomplish, which helped tremendously with garnering community acceptance. This two-hour encounter helped us both understand each other, to see the misrepresentations and misunderstandings that stemmed from entrenched positions of fear and suspicion.

I was reminded once again of the hospitality to visitors that Islam teaches. As for the Ayatollah, maybe his preconceived notion of the relationship between the international aid community and the occupying forces was shifted just a little. I couldn't blame him for seeing all Western actors as puppets of their governments. While largely stemming from his personal experience within a totalitarian government, it wasn't helped when billions in aid funds were spent on projects that were not requested by the people who these projects were meant to assist—the Iraqis.

Divine intervention

Seven years after my visit to Ayatollah Sheikh Bashir, I was aboard a Boeing 737 headed to Najaf. The nearly two-hour flight was uneventful. I kept to myself, blending in; my southern European features and an obligatory, perfectly trimmed, seven-day growth helped detract attention. On the inside, though, my stomach was curdling.

As we broke through the clouds to begin the final descent I caught a full panoramic view of the city and the largest graveyard in the world, the place where the final wishes of the Shia faithful—to be buried near Imam Ali—are fulfilled. Founded in the eighth century, Najaf traces its provenance to the whim of a camel carrying the dead body of Ali, the slain forebear of the Shia, and the namesake of the shrine built upon the ground at which the camel eventually came to rest. From the air it seems the camel had a good eye. I could see how centuries ago it would have been a wise place to establish a settlement—close to a water source and with one half of the approach to the city protected by the Sea of Najaf. Maybe the camel had been guided by God.

Divine intervention is a closely held belief amongst Muslims, most evidently expressed in the common remark in Arabic, *insha'allah*, meaning 'God willing'. It's used in various ways including as an affirmative response, as in, 'Can I please have a receipt for that?'

'Insha'allah' is said as the receipt is handed over.

It's also commonly used to pass off responsibility by speaking the word while responding with a smile and nod even though knowing the truth to be otherwise.

Saddam's soldier #1 shouts, 'We will chase the infidels into the sea!'

Saddam's soldier #2, smiling, may have responded, 'Insha'allah.'

I've rarely heard it used in its purest form—if God is willing then this highly unlikely outcome that we all hope and pray for could well come true.

A few kilometres east of the outskirts of Najaf is Kufa, another religious city with historical roots, and to the north, Karbala, home to two more Shia shrines. This cluster of three cities is at the heart of the divisions between Sunni and Shia Islam, representing what Islamic State, the Sunni militant fundamentalists that swept through Iraq in 2014, find so abhorrent. The division began with the passing of Prophet Mohammad and the concern over who should lead the community. Some argued that the closest relative, his cousin, Ali, and husband to the Prophet's daughter, Fatima, should lead while others looked to the older and earlier follower of Mohammad, his father-in-law, Abu Bakr. It was the latter who won the support of the community, leading them for a brief two years before passing away. Umar followed Abu Bakr. Then in 656 AD the third Caliph, Uthman, was assassinated, with varying accusations emerging of Ali's role in his death. This eventually led to Ali's ascension to the leadership and the title of Caliph. The accusations and divisions left deep wounds between those who saw Uthman's demise as the result of Ali's machinations and those who thought Ali had been designated successor by Mohammad in the first place. The result was continuing conflict and the first civil war within the Islamic community.

Nearly fifteen hundred years later those defining historical events remain fresh, often kept alive through religious commemorations such as the Day of Ashura, a solemn religious occasion reminding Shia of the death of Hussein, Ali's son, at the hands of the supporters of Uthman's successors. It is common for Sunnis to name their children Umar or Uthman—Shia will not. The veneration of Shia Imams and their shrines is seen as idolatry by some Sunnis. As a result, Sunni extremists such as Islamic State have destroyed Shia shrines while many Iraqis carry different ID cards with names appropriate for Sunni and Shia regions.

In the Middle East wars are fought because of religion. History is shaped by religion. Borders are drawn with religion in mind. Political parties are based on religion. Governments rise and fall on the back of religious rulings. Religion is in the architecture, the art, the language, the music, and even the ground where the sacred stands apart from the profane.

Understanding religion is fundamental to understanding the Middle East, from the poetic literature to cultural nuances to views on charitable giving including who are the needy and how societies recover after wars. More fundamentally it contributes to the principles that form a logic that seems illogical to outsiders.

For most Iraqi Muslims, religious beliefs and the divine are not only a reason to live, but also a way to live. In the early days as the IRC was setting up operations in Najaf, the war photographer, Peter Biro, was sent out to document our work. Long before the era of kidnapping aid workers, foreigners would jog along the streets for exercise and Western females would wear 'things which could not be politely described'. During one of his jogs Peter was stopped by a man sitting in a doorway. Seeing foreigners in Najaf was a rare sight so the man rolled his hand in the common gesture meaning, 'what are you doing?'

'Jogging,' Peter replied, pumping his hands vigorously in the universal symbol for the exercise. Shocked and clearly misunderstanding the situation, the man leaned forward, vigorously shaking his pointed finger, and shouted, 'No dancing, no dancing!' Dancing is considered by some scholars as un-Islamic as is, depending upon whom you ask, chess, laughter, and music. It wouldn't have taken much to figure out that in Najaf, America's hopes for an open, pluralistic, tolerant Iraq would come up against a formidable brick wall.

As my plane began its descent into Najaf, I remembered being reminded of this clash of cultures every morning as I'd tune in to Radio Sawa, a US government funded soft diplomacy effort to spread pop culture in Iraq, and would be greeted with tunes such as 'Rock Your Body' by Justin Timberlake.

As an Australian I needed a visa to enter any part of Iraq outside of the northern Kurdish region. Firas had promised to help facilitate a visa when I first raised the idea of returning, but by the time the idea became reality, he had already emigrated to the US, leaving behind the turmoil of his homeland. Haider, who had come with Firas and me on our first visit to the Ayatollah, was now my point of contact in Najaf. We'd kept in touch via email mainly on matters related to his application for refugee status in the United States. As with Firas he had applied using a visa established for Iraqis who had been associated with American military units, NGOs, media and contractors—a setup replicated by the Australian government for Iraqi and Afghan support staff who had helped the Australian mission—its availability due to such staff being particularly vulnerable to persecution for supporting the occupation. As the point of contact verifying the employment status of staff who were applying for this special category of US visas, I knew that it was only the educated middle class that were emigrating. The poor and illiterate, the guards, drivers, cooks, and cleaners who we had employed and were at equal risk wouldn't have known how to complete the application forms.

While Haider was seeking my help in getting him out of the country, I was relying on him to get back in. He had promised to arrange a seven-day pass from the passport office in the Najaf Airport, though I had no paperwork to prove it. I wasn't quite sure what the consequences were for illegally entering the country. I hoped it was no more than a slap on the wrist and being put on the next flight back, and tried not to think of the other possibilities.

Being the third most important destination on a devout Shia Muslim's travel itinerary makes an airport crucial infrastructure. Amazingly, Najaf did not have an airport until mid-2008 when a Kuwaiti firm's efforts at rehabilitating an old air force base opened the city for the first time to international travellers.

The airport, built in an old-fashioned hangar style, is secure, modern, clean, and very spacious, but none of that was on my mind as I walked to Immigration. Instead, I began to look around for someone, anyone, who looked familiar. Where was Haider's contact? Did he forget? Maybe his promise of a visa was all bluster, not believing that I would actually come. Then to my surprise a very young woman appeared in front of me covered in the customary black abaya worn in religiously conservative areas. With a beaming smile framed by her hijab, she introduced herself as Zahra.

'Please follow me,' she said cheerfully.

Zahra, as it turns out, worked at Immigration. She was a former staff member of IRO, the local organisation that I had helped set up before I left Iraq in 2005. She seemed to have that unique ability to perfectly balance the cultural reservedness expected of women while still being assertive and able to get her message across. Her nonchalance about the whole situation slowly began to put me at ease. While she was enthusiastic to help, it seemed that getting an entry visa upon arrival would not be such an easy thing. I was shown a seat and asked to wait. Haider was brought in from the arrivals area to answer for me. Five years had passed since I'd seen him last and it showed. He'd added some weight in all the wrong places, along with a few more grey hairs. A pair of reading glasses had been added to his shirt pocket. Time hadn't changed his fashion sense, though, as he was dressed in the common Iraqi style— an oversized suit, perfectly polished shoes and no tie.

Zahra, meanwhile was on the phone to a senior immigration officer. There was a lot of hand waving and hand shaking. Then it all seemed to be settled. A solution was found. I just needed to confirm that I was a pilgrim visiting the Shrine of Imam Ali.

I responded with a smile and answered, 'Insha'allah.'

* * *

After passing Immigration I was soon sitting in the backseat of Haider's car on the way into the city, my initial fears and trepidation quickly forgotten as memories of the familiar streets slowly returned. With Haider behind the wheel and his brother with us, we chatted as they took me on a tour of Najaf, driving in a relatively new Hyundai Sonata with import papers still plastered across the windows (I was told this adds to the resale value). As we passed other cars I swivelled my head each time to see if the passengers were correctly configured—in conservative cities there is a specific order to how men and women are seated to prevent being tempted into licentious behaviour. A husband and wife could sit side by side at the front, but a man and a woman who weren't related would need to sit separately; the man driving and the woman in the back seat. Two women and one man would see both women in the back and the man driving. Two men and two women is easy. But that's for sedans. In Iraq, single cab pick-ups are common, in which case the men sit in the front while the women are in the back tray.

Our former office building looked derelict, but driving by brought back memories of times when it was full of activity. The entrance to the sprawling undercover downtown market was as spectacular as I remembered it. After an hour of driving we pulled into my favourite restaurant, recently renovated and renamed Al Rawan Restaurant for Tourists. I suspect the term 'tourists' referred to Iranians as I couldn't imagine too many Western backpackers kicking up their feet and ordering a beer. As we entered I was reminded yet again of the segregation of the sexes: there was the main area for single men and then a closed off, air-conditioned room for families. We sat in the single males area, though in the past my colleagues had thought it appropriate that we sit in the family area since I was a foreigner, which somehow made it appropriate.

Eating out Iraqi style is a hurried affair where food is served promptly and devoured just as quickly. The traditional cuisine is rich and varied, with my favourite being the Najafi/Iranian specialty, *fesenjoon*, a pomegranate-based sauce served with strips of cooked chicken. Regrettably though, Iraq's restaurants only offer a standard menu of quick-to-prepare dishes—kebab, shawarma or tikka. Slow dining is yet to come to Iraq.

I kept in time with my fellow diners, putting the conversation on hold and scoffing the food without taking a breath. Following custom, as soon as we finished eating we left our mess behind, washed our hands in the bathroom, and then moved to an empty table to have tea. All the while I sauntered through the restaurant as if I was born a Najafi.

Drinking tea in Iraq is a versatile affair. It can be taken at the breakfast table, in the office, at a restaurant or while lounging on a sofa watching television. Chai, as it is known in Arabic, is served to a double espresso measure in a glass the shape of a voluptuous woman. Often flavoured with cardamom, the tea is roughly one-part sugar to five parts water and is served scorching hot, even when the temperature outside is over forty degrees.

As we sat and talked I was reminded of how quickly Haider's children had grown. His two eldest I remembered: a daughter then aged eleven and a ten-year-old boy, but his youngest, only five years old, hadn't been born when we last saw each other. Their ages meant lives that had only known war. What impact would this have on them? With their futures in mind, Haider had applied for refugee status in America in the hope of giving his children a better start in life. His dream was to follow in the footsteps of millions of others who had gone to America over the past centuries seeking opportunity. I asked him why he was leaving behind a country in which he had a respectable job, his qualifications were recognised and the culture and religion were familiar—everything that he would lose by moving to America.

'I will not lose anything in this big step. I will consider it a chance and if this chance brings a benefit for my family, that will be better and I will win finally. But, if not, it will be like a beautiful trip that I took with my family to spend in the most beautiful place in the world.'

Of course, Haider didn't literally think that America was the most beautiful place in the world. America had become a metaphor for a utopia representing what many Iraqis aspired to. For some it was beautiful because of the economic opportunities; for those fleeing persecution the promise of safety made it so, and to others it was simply the land of plenty where you didn't need to work hard to live the good life.

'In Iraq we don't enjoy our rights like those in other Arab countries. We are living in a country disrupted by continuous wars and conflicts. Which is better? To stay in this country and subject you and your family to serious danger, or search for another chance for security and generous living for your family?' asked Haider. I couldn't fault the logic but wondered what would happen to the country and those left behind when the educated and capable people like Haider leave the country.

I was also reminded, as we reminisced, that Haider was kidnapped on the same day that Fadi was taken. While we mobilised to secure the expatriate's release, including bringing in a kidnap and ransom specialist, Haider and his colleague Wissam fell by the wayside in the mayhem, leaving their families to barter for their freedom. Looking back, I'm sorry for the part I played in neglecting their situation.

Having finished the tea, we got down to business. The agenda for my visit was packed as I only planned to stay four days, hoping to be in and out before word got around that there was an unarmed, unprotected Australian wandering about town. First up was a meeting with Grand Ayatollah Sheikh Bashir. The Ayatollah's office had set the appointment for eight-thirty pm, around the same time as our previous meeting, leaving me to wonder whether he got a kick out of having me travel through the eerie streets of downtown Najaf at night. Thursday and Friday were allocated to visiting projects such as the first women's centre in Najaf, two water treatment plants, and the main hospital. We'd chosen these as they were relatively close to town, as well as being a representative mix of the different areas of work we had previously been engaged in. On the last day a reunion with former IRC colleagues was scheduled in the morning, minimising the time that any loose tongues could create problems and then I would be back to the airport, ready to return home.

Tales from an Ayatollah

The sleeping quarters I was allocated were in a renovated house used as office space for the local Najafi NGO, Iraqi Relief Organisation (IRO). As with most Iraqi houses, there were two entrances ensuring that cultural norms could be met: one for the family, women in particular, which usually opens into the kitchen, and another for guests, leading to the communal lounge room. As it had been converted into an office, all the staff and guests walked through the kitchen before entering the main work area, a two-storey foyer.

As I walked in and was introduced to the staff, my eyes wandered to the photos and notices plastered on every available wall space. It was an amazing two-storey resume showcasing the successes of an Iraqi civil society group that was only established in 2005. Haider proudly told me they had secured over two-million dollars' worth of funding from international donors, spending it on nearly sixty projects across Najaf.

IRO was established from the remnants of the IRC's activities in Najaf. Headquarters had decided to shut down operations after three kidnappings and two staff deaths, while the lack of a looming humanitarian crisis made the risks disproportionate to the benefits. At the time I was against the decision to withdraw as I knew how fickle the situation was and could see the potential for a rapid escalation of violence and the inevitable humanitarian crisis that follows. Since we had done the hard work of establishing trust within a community, I didn't think that it was the time to throw it all away to only come back in a few years (as happened) and start from scratch. As the country director I flew to New York to lobby headquarters on the importance of remaining operational, but to no avail. There was a view among a small minority that we couldn't be neutral in circumstances where we were so closely tied to the belligerent forces.

We closed operations on 31 December 2004, handing over assets situated in Najaf to the newly minted IRO. Many of the Najaf-based Iraqi senior staff volunteered their time to the new organisation until project funding was found. It didn't take long for money to come, which was no surprise considering the organisation was led by Iraqis who had proven they could operate under the most difficult environments, understood the needs of the people, and were able to satisfy the bureaucratic demands of international donors. But with the emigration of Firas and Haider along with other senior staff, the organisation folded in 2011, a practical example of the impact upon war-torn societies when the best and brightest, mainly from the middle class, seek refuge away from their home country.

I continued walking along the montaged walls, feeling buoyed by the obvious success of this group. On exhibit along the walls were lists of water pipes laid, tables of humanitarian aid packages distributed, photos of anti-corruption symposiums held, and maps showing health facilities constructed. It was an impressive operation that had clearly endeared itself to the community in this unique city. Among the montage I found two projects Firas had proudly told me about some time ago: a distribution of humanitarian goods to a group of over four thousand families and the expansion of a school overwhelmed by new students who had been displaced by the civil war.

Following the February 2006 bombing of an historic Shia mosque by Sunni extremists in Samarra, just north of Baghdad, civil war broke out. The Sunnis who had lived in Shia neighbourhoods fled to Sunni areas and the Shia likewise fled to their strongholds. An estimated 1.6 million people left their homes to seek safety in homogenous communities. Over a period of a year, nearly sixty thousand headed to Najaf where Firas and his team were operating. In response, IRO received funds from various international donors to provide assistance; one such activity was the distribution of humanitarian goods to families. The packages distributed to each family included twenty-five kilograms of rice, five kilograms of lentils, two litres of oil, two kilograms of detergents, and a dozen bars of soap. In addition, they provided essential non-food items such as blankets, mattresses, a fan, straw mat, clothes, towels, and a torch. Chai was not forgotten—one kilogram of tea leaves and an incredible ten kilograms of sugar completed the package.

To the uninitiated, distributing humanitarian packages may sound as pleasant as dressing up as Santa during Christmas, but it isn't. Preventing fraud, ensuring order, bringing together the logistics in the middle of a war zone along with never having enough to meet the need—all this can be incredibly challenging, risky, and heartbreaking. That IRO managed not once but on numerous occasions to successfully organise a distribution during a civil war, while numerous militias were rampaging throughout the country, is a testament to the quality of its staff.

The second project was the expansion of the Al Gheri primary school. The arrival of tens of thousands of displaced families into Najaf created a tremendous strain on services, in particular health and education. For the students and teachers at Al Gheri School, their already full classrooms had to squeeze in more students. A classroom made for thirty or forty students had to cope with over fifty hustling for a space to sit, two to a chair in some cases.

In response IRO managed the construction of a second floor with an additional three classrooms. They sourced funding, brought the local authorities on board, worked with the department of education to ensure that additional teachers were assigned, and received sign off from the engineering department.

As the hustle and bustle of the office continued despite my arrival, I was shown upstairs to where I'd be spending the next four nights. Looking for easy exits had become second nature when moving into new accommodation. I immediately noticed that there was no way out—no balcony, no accessible window, not even a good place to hide if something were to happen. I looked around the second floor for the usual staircase to the roof: nothing. Despite the uncomfortable feeling that this wasn't the safest place to be I had to accept it and move on to planning for the forthcoming meeting.

As evening fell I started preparing for my meeting with the Ayatollah. It had been nearly seven years since we last met and I felt like Dorothy off to see the Wizard of Oz. The tune from the movie popped into my mind, and I hummed along, I'm off to see the Ayatollah, the wonderful Ayatollah of Najaf. This being Najaf where dogs were considered dirty we didn't have Toto, nevertheless I had Haider and his friend Kadhim accompanying me to the old town. The most notable change I saw as we wound through the same streets that led us toward the Ayatollah's compound all those years ago was an absence of weapons and marauding militiamen. The only armed men were the Iraqi police standing at strategic corners keeping the peace between the sometimes volatile clerical factions, each with their own militia and some with murderous reputations.

Upon our arrival at the Ayatollah's compound, the routine followed the old script: we were stopped at the gate, searched at the door, took off our shoes, and then shown to the welcoming room. Just as we sat cross-legged on the floor the lights went off. While security had returned to Najaf, neither the Americans nor the Iraqi government could solve the pressing problem of the greatly increased demand for electricity, mainly a result of new household air conditioners, so the blight of blackouts continued.

Using my phone to illuminate the space, I could see that the interior of the still sparsely furnished room hadn't changed. The same bookshelf was there but in a different corner. A worn carpet adorned the floor, though I couldn't say if it was the same one as before. I suspected there were pictures hanging on the walls, but my makeshift torch didn't light that far ahead. Robed and turbaned men whisked past us in the shadows. It seemed surreal, ghostly, as if the wraiths from a Harry Potter movie had come alive.

As my eyes adjusted to the dark, Basim Ali, the head of the Ayatollah's charitable foundation, joined us. Basim is a highly astute man, someone you'd want on your team, and certainly had I the chance I would have partnered with his organisation. However, working with overtly religious Muslim NGOs is complicated by a Western donor anxiety that they are fronts for terrorists. The fear is that the resources will be diverted to 'unsavoury' purposes, namely the funding of associated political and military bodies. When I discussed this with my staff, they would point out the long history of organisations such as the Muslim Brotherhood, Hamas and Hezbollah in providing grass-roots social services and the even longer history of religious leaders having charitable responsibilities. The debate is a chicken and egg argument. Do the militant organisations create a dependency upon their welfare and social services so that they can ensure a steady stream of new recruits to channel into their militant wings? Or do these welfare organisations transform into armed political movements as a response to corruption, rising inequality and an ambition for social justice? The reality is probably a combination of both. As I was thinking about this the electricity returned and within moments the Ayatollah entered the room.

As he entered we all quickly rose, though I was a little slower to get up—my knees not being used to sitting crossed-legged for so long. One after the other we all kissed the hand of the Ayatollah—this time it felt the right thing to do—before returning to the cushions.

He'd lost a lot of weight. Everything else was the same—the clothes, the worn prayer rug complexion, the black-rimmed glasses. It was as if it was yesterday and he was shaking his finger threateningly at me. The Ayatollah's son introduced us once again, and a flicker of recognition passed across his face as he looked squarely at me. I presumed that he recalled my previous visit, though it was hard to say and an uncomfortable question to ask. Then the floor was handed over to me. Just like last time, working through a translator in addition to the formality of meeting an Iraqi religious leader meant that we both ended up communicating in monologues, delivering speeches rather than participating in a flowing exchange of words.

'Thank you for welcoming me. I am now visiting alone, without an organisation, on a personal journey to see what happened to our work and whether it helped the people.' I paused, allowing Haider to translate, then continued, 'It has been a long time since we met, but I have always looked back on our first meeting with fond memories. Many of your words have stayed with me since then, in particular the parable of Prophet Mohammad escorting the Christian to his home.'

Silence. Blank stares were shared between Basim, Haider and the others. I didn't know what I had said wrong. As it was translated the Ayatollah alone seemed to know what I was talking about and corrected me, saying, 'It was Imam Ali who accompanied the Christian.' Mortified by my mistake it took me a moment to recover. Not quite the start I had hoped for. Nevertheless, I ploughed ahead.

Hoping to find out whether his opinions of foreign aid organisations had changed, but not wanting to remind him of his earlier position, I asked an open-ended question: 'What contribution do you think foreign aid organisations can make to Iraq?' He turned the question around by asking me, 'What contribution do you think you made?'

'I'm yet to visit the old projects, but I suspect that the greatest contribution we made was building human capital.' This idea had dominated my thoughts since earlier in the afternoon as I read about one project after another and marvelled at what IRO had accomplished, never imagining that they would be so successful. The idea developed further as I listened to stories of staff, now politicians or senior government officials, who credited their personal success to their time working with us. Nawal, our former health education officer whom I planned to meet the next day, had entered politics and won the largest number of votes of any female politician during the provincial elections. Qasem, our former logistics officer, joined the Iraqi version of the FBI, claiming to have passed the tests off the back of his experience with us; and another staff member, Farouk, had become the chief engineer in a major garments manufacturing company. Maybe their praise was just polite chatter, but I ran with it.

'Few people in Najaf could operate a computer or write in English. Now, several years later, having a local organisation such as IRO raising funds from the international community, operating its own projects or seeing ex-staff as politicians representing the people, is probably the best contribution.'

The Ayatollah nodded, his face emotionless, adding his own take on our contribution that was translated in tandem by Basim and Haider. 'In general, foreign organisations didn't submit real assistance for people in Iraq. They provided service only for displaced people, not covering and focusing on the most affected slices of the community, the orphans and widows, who are the victims of wars and conflicts. There are thousands of orphans who should be provided with more assistance from international organisations.' I wanted to respond by explaining that we couldn't choose who we would help, as the US government had restricted our funding to the displaced. However, this would only exacerbate his suspicions of NGOs so I left it at that. Nor did I point out that his focus on orphans and widows likely stemmed from a literal reading of the Koran and Hadith and didn't necessarily mean that they were the most in need.

Suddenly he lapsed into another parable. 'Imam Ali was known to wear summer clothes during winter and winter clothes during summer so that he could understand the plight of the people.' For a few moments I felt myself growing frustrated at his diverging off the topic. But I quickly realised that the Ayatollah had captured the key dilemma of international aid work. To what extent should we live in the shoes of the people rather than focusing our energies on getting a job done? I have had postings where my home was a bare building with no running water or electricity, living as others from the community did, but the result was limited working hours and exhaustion during the summer heat. Alternatively, I've had access to generators and a borehole in the compound that led to improved efficiency but not necessarily effectiveness.

I remembered some lighter moments that illustrated the gist of his tale, such as when a foreign official who had spent little time outside of the walled compounds in Baghdad jumped out of fear as a hail of gunfire could be heard just outside of my offices. I quickly reassured him that it was celebratory gunfire probably related to the international soccer match Iraq was playing that day. I learned to make these quick calls through a mix of being a part of local society and knowing what was on people's minds, along with quick glances to Iraqis on the street to see how they were reacting. There were also more serious reminders. For the thousands of Iraqis and few foreigners who lived outside of the Green Zone, but worked or had business in the enclave where the international Coalition and Iraqi government were based, entering meant lining up in plain sight of snipers and at risk of car bombs. It was a daily dice with death that ended up costing many lives. While little more could have been done to prevent it, few of the people calling meetings in the Green Zone recognised the risk we took every time we responded to their calls.

My mind wandered, imagining Western government officials contemplating the parable's implications as they dined in various American fast food joints during the year or two spent in Iraq without ever leaving the Green Zone. Could they really understand the plight of the people and make decisions on their behalf by simply reading reports? I recalled the Baghdad-based project officer I met, in charge of the US Agency for International Development's largest community-based development program, studying Latin in his off-time. He thought learning Arabic was irrelevant and unnecessary.

'Does it matter who is providing the aid? Does it matter if it is from the United Nations, NGOs, or other groups?' I asked, fully focused once again. The Ayatollah responded, 'It doesn't matter who is providing the aid, as long as the people are honest people. You need honest people to represent you. You need honest people to guide you when working in a new culture.'

The next question came hesitantly as I knew the Ayatollah's position towards the United States and the invasion of 2003. In fact, I was so cautious I decided to also subsequently submit these questions in writing to ensure that the response was not misrepresented or mistranslated. 'What are your thoughts on humanitarian aid being delivered by a military that is responsible for the conflict? For example, immediately after the US invasion, was it okay that the US military was involved in providing humanitarian assistance?'

'It should be clear,' came the written response reflecting what he had said at the meeting, 'that the objective of such activity by the army is not to serve the people, but it is to deceive the public and poor people, in order to misguide the people and to seize their nation and creed, their wealth and means, their land and airspace, everything, with the goal to make them their slaves; just as Yazeed, Ubaidullah ibn Ziyad, Umar ibn Saad and such cursed people deceived the people of Iraq in the same way and made them prepared to fight against Imam Husayn.'

The Ayatollah was referencing a time in the late seventh century when the followers of Imam Ali were struggling to retain their claim to being the true heirs to the new religion. History, it seems, is not forgotten so long as it continues to serve its purpose.

He continued, 'This has always been the practice of the temporal despotic powers. Therefore, it is the religious and patriotic duty of every person of intellect, possessor of a conscience, carrier of esteem and magnanimity, to avoid such deception.'

What mattered to me and to many aid agencies working in Afghanistan, Iraq, Yemen or any other country on the frontline of the clash between Islamic militants and the West was whether we are justified targets or neutral actors. I asked about the more publicly visible money trail: 'Does it matter where the money for humanitarian aid comes from? For example, during the US invasion many NGOs got money from the US government, does that matter?'

'All these organisations have a duty not to take part in such activities by which there is detriment to the religion of Islam, or if it results in the damage of freedom in an Islamic country or by which the enemy of the state and Islam gains further strength, even if it may be to simply send money,' he responded, holding his fists firmly on his lap, the sentences issuing forth from his mouth like small bullets.

The message was clear. He saw us as aiding and abetting the US military in its mission to 'seize the nation'. A different argument but built upon the same intellectual foundation as the views expressed at IRC headquarters by those who argued for the mission to be closed down. Arguably the second most powerful ayatollah in Iraq was emphasising that humanitarian organisations must not receive funding from the United States if they are to operate as neutral actors in his country.

Many NGOs have had this ethical debate internally. Some, such as Oxfam, opted against receiving Coalition funding during the Iraq war while others, such as IRC, chose to only take money that didn't come with too many strings attached. The early aid contracts with the US government had some constraining clauses that raised eyebrows and frustrated NGOs, including, 'all contact with the news media, in Washington or overseas, must be approved and coordinated by the USAID Press Office'. These media restrictions stymied organisations from advocating on humanitarian issues during the war, undoubtedly succeeding in buying the silence of some.

Since then the strings attached to US government aid money made the earlier clauses seem quaint. New obligations have transformed charities into extensions of the military or 'force multipliers'—a term used by Colin Powell to describe NGOs. Extracts from more recent contracts from Afghanistan show that charities are now expected to 'support military efforts in communities by helping to "hold" areas after they are cleared', to provide 'direct support of ongoing and planned USG counterinsurgency efforts', or to 'implement program activities...in post-battlefield clean-up operations'. I understood the Ayatollah's suspicion very well.

I was still processing what the Ayatollah had said when he asked me, 'How do people in your country receive aid?'

'Through the government,' I said. 'We pay taxes, which are then redirected through social services and to the people in need.'

'What we do,' he answered, referring to his organisation, 'is the same.' He was referring to how his followers would pay zakat, which would then be collected by his organisation and distributed to people in need.

The conversation continued among the gathered group in Arabic before Haider looked toward me, raising his eyebrows, suggesting that unless I had any other questions it would be polite to leave. I thanked the Ayatollah for his time, and we started to stand up. Just as we were leaving the room he added a few words. 'I'm sure it's not what you wanted to hear. It's hard to hear such things.' He was right; it wasn't what I wanted to hear, but it was what I had expected. We had grown up in cultures far too different for the Ayatollah and I to find much common ground, but nevertheless it was time well spent sitting together listening to each other's perspectives.

Passing by religious scholars and followers, we headed back onto the dimly lit streets of the old city and then on to the IRO offices where I bunkered down for the night.

Cause and effect

Surprisingly I slept like a baby. There was no gunfire and I didn't feel any sense of trepidation. The only thing that woke me through the night was the stifling heat and the old and noisy air conditioner that I had to keep turning on as it got too hot and then off as it got too cold. Sleeping downstairs were an unarmed guard and Haider, who told his wife and family that while I was visiting he wouldn't be coming home—a gesture that I greatly appreciated.

I was lost in my thoughts as we drove to the entrance of the Al Zahra Women's Centre in the Al Manathara Quarter of Najaf, only a few minutes from the IRO office. Two guards were casually lounging about the entrance of the building, seemingly enjoying the morning sun before the day heated up. Still suspicious of Haider's assessment of the security situation, I mumbled my Arabic greetings, shook hands firmly and then placed my right hand on my heart to show pleasure in meeting them, and then shuffled past. It was all done quickly so that no opportunity was left for a conversation. Once inside the single-storey building, figuring the women of the centre wouldn't have a militia or criminal gang on quick dial, I relaxed a little.

The centre was headed by Um Tiba. The 'Um' is an honorific that together with 'Tiba' means 'Mother of Tiba'. In the Arab world, once parents have children they are no longer referred to by their first names, but rather as 'father of' or 'mother of' the eldest child.

If the eldest is a girl and the second or any subsequent child a boy, then the parents go by the boy's name.

Um Tiba appeared to be a strong-willed woman, directing the men at every turn, eager for the opportunity to display the successes she had forged and equally unafraid to highlight the centre's bleak future. Dressed in the traditional abaya, she didn't stand out amidst the other women apart from her white hijab with blue polka dots, which seemed somewhat daring to me. She led us into her cramped offices where we were offered a customary drink, which was thankfully not tea as I was already riding a sugar high after having had several so far. The room itself was in need of renovation as was the rest of the building, or as many Iraqis would say in their language, it all looked 'tired'. It had clearly been a house in its previous incarnation and we were probably sitting in a child's bedroom. That Um Tiba had chosen the smallest room in the house for her office made her different. She was daring and humble. I liked her.

After a series of courteous words in Arabic I began the conversation in English. 'I was working here in Najaf six years ago with the IRC team,' I said, indicating at Haider and Farouq who were accompanying me during this visit. It seemed Um Tiba understood some English so I continued but made an extra effort to enunciate more clearly while Haider continued to translate just in case some of the message was lost. 'I'm visiting the places where we used to work to see what happened to the projects.'

She seemed nonplussed by my return and accepted my probing into the past without question. Only Qasem, the intelligence officer, had shown any surprise at my arrival in Najaf, telling me that I was a hero for returning and praising me for my continued interest in Iraq, but then quickly admonishing me for not having adequate protection and clearing it with the government's security apparatus first.

'The Zahra centre was the first women's centre in Najaf,' Um Tiba began proudly, opening with the strengths as any good salesperson would. 'We provide training to women on computers, sewing, hairdressing, and business. As you can see we are very popular with women of Najaf.' If the number of women milling about the property were an indication, she was right; there were at least a hundred members present that day.

'Was the centre already in operation when the IRC partnered with you?' I asked, as I didn't remember all the details. 'Or did we help establish it from scratch?'

'The centre,' she answered, 'was established in 2003 by the Department of Youth, but we had no equipment and nothing to do. They gave us the building and paid salaries for the staff. Then IRC started to provide support.'

'If we didn't help what would the situation be like here, how would it be different?' I asked as bodies came and went through the cramped office seemingly without any regard for our meeting. I was struggling to catch all of Haider's translation even though he was sitting right next to me as the lectures and hands-on learning in the other rooms was so loud.

The translation was slow, so I peeked out of the corner of my eye at the traffic in the adjacent room. It was a busy area full of abaya-clad women moving around from one room to another. I suspect that had we not come the women would only be covered in the hijab, but unfortunately for them men were in the office and that meant putting on the heavy synthetic head-to-toe covering, stifling in the summer heat of Najaf.

'We would sit in this building without doing any work,' was what eventually came back as a response to my question.

I returned back to the positive, asking, 'How many women have benefited from the last six years of service?'

'About a million,' she answered. The figure seemed absurd, so I asked again, but was given the same answer. Seeing that I wasn't convinced, she gave out instructions and within seconds an assistant came in with a pile of registration forms containing no more than several hundred pages. Maybe she meant a metaphorical million.

'Would you like a tour?'

I was surprised by the offer as I thought that most of the centre would be off limits to men, but I quickly accepted. We were taken through the building—a single-storey ageing structure probably built in the seventies before Saddam's rise and the subsequent troubles that accompanied his ascent. From the computer training room to where the sewing machines were lined up to the most popular class, the hairdressing salon, it seemed the house was full to the brim. At each stop I could see the women hurriedly tightening their hijabs and tucking away any loose strands of hair before we entered. I greeted each group with the customary 'Salam aleikhum'. The aspiring hairdressers, as with the other classes, didn't seem to be receiving hands-on training as twenty or thirty sat in rows of chairs staring intently forwards. Instead, the women watched as an instructor held up different tools of the hairdressing trade and presumably explained what each was for.

The last room we visited was, surprisingly, an exercise room. Apparently, though I could only roughly judge the weight of the women through the shape-standardising abaya, a lot of Najafi women were overweight.

'Doctors send women to the centre to learn how to exercise,' Um Tiba explained.

'Is it a popular class?' I asked.

'Yes, one of the most popular, because women do not have a chance to exercise outside,' she told us, though we all knew this very well. The result of this religious expectation has been catastrophic for women's health, with a World Health Organization report finding that 38% of Iraqi women were obese.

As we continued the tour I asked, 'Do women benefit from the training by getting jobs after they graduate?' She initially said yes, but after some further questions the answer was no. There were no jobs for women who learned a skill through this centre. Unless a woman gained a degree from a university, outside employment opportunities were limited. This didn't mean that the benefit of having an alternative place for women to meet and socialise wasn't important. Other than their homes and their friends' houses, women in Iraq have few places to mix openly without their men accompanying them. However, it did not seem to correlate to employment.

It is difficult to quantify the benefit to the women. Those attending hairdressing classes were unlikely to do any hairdressing work, but they were learning, participating, engaging and socialising. But this is at the heart of the problem with today's aid industry: any planned initiative must have measurable means to gauge its impact, such as improving outcomes in household income, literacy, child mortality or gender-based violence. For women's centres such as Al Zahra, the primary benefit is intuitive but difficult and very costly to measure—giving the women of Najaf a safe place to meet to build a sense of confidence and independence doesn't translate into measurable units.

In each of the rooms we passed I saw piles of equipment that we had provided seven years ago, which had since broken down or worn out. Broken sports equipment in an outside shed, covered computer equipment, and even the generator that another organisation had provided were all broken. Um Tiba made her concerns clear to me: 'If we don't get new funding there will be nothing for the women to do and they will stop coming'. She said this without a hint of exaggeration.

The Department of Youth, for reasons of their own, had decided to support the establishment of another women's centre in 2009, which received government funds to equip its facilities. The Al Zahra centre had not been successful in receiving any government funds other than ongoing salary support. Sadly, it seemed inevitable that in a few months or a year this centre could be empty of women for lack of any functioning equipment.

We headed back to the entrance. 'Thank you for showing us this wonderful centre that has benefited so much from all of the hard work you and your team put into it,' I said sincerely, seeing how much it was appreciated by the women there that day.

'Please, tell your friends that we need help. We need more support to continue helping the women of Najaf,' Um Tiba said in a plea whose message came across clearly even though it was in Arabic.

The conversation that consumed my thoughts as we walked into the women's centre an hour or so prior took centre stage again as we left. What matters is what is left behind. In the case of the Al Zahra centre, a functioning women's facility was left behind in 2003, but seven years later, without government or community support, it was deteriorating and on the verge of collapse. Is it right to establish a women's centre that gives its members a taste of a new life, only to have it taken away a few years later because society doesn't consider it a priority? Are there better ways to contribute to sustained cultural change? And even if there were, is that our business? Maybe a seed had been planted in the minds of the Najafi people, one that would eventually sprout a realisation that having a centre is not corrupting of women's morals. Maybe one of the women from the centre would rise above the fray and enter the political sphere with newfound confidence to lead a social revolution. If this was to occur, at least it would be driven from within the community, giving any change a stronger chance of establishing itself.

But such a wait-and-see approach isn't how the aid industry is structured. Instead, there is a forcefulness, a cultural imperialism, that is pushed just as much by individuals as by the system. When I first arrived in Najaf, two American female staff refused to cover their heads with a hijab. Their view was that the hijab was a sign of female oppression and a cultural relic that needed to change in line with the new Iraq. They wanted change then and there. The problem was that their views only created resentment among the many Iraqi women who were pushing the boundaries of social acceptability at their own pace by, for example, working alongside men and they didn't need the extra attention and anger that the two women were generating, which risked a pushback and a possible loss of limited gains that they had achieved.

***

Next stop—Al Sadr hospital or as it's alternatively known, the Najaf Teaching Hospital. The differing names are more than a matter of semantics, much like the words used to describe the events of March 2003: 'invasion' or 'liberation'? For the religious, it's Al Sadr, recalling the name of Muqtadr's relatives and forebears, a family of Islamic scholars and leaders who were persecuted by Saddam Hussein; while the secular tend to call it the Teaching Hospital.

The seven-storey sandstone coloured building housing the hospital lies just off the main road leading into Najaf. It is the largest medical facility in southern Iraq and, as one of its names suggests, a major teaching hospital. The hospital, located immediately to the west of the former CPA compound, between Najaf and the satellite city of Kufa, became a battle zone in the First Najaf Civil War. During the conflict in early 2004, the Mehdi Militia used the higher ground afforded by the hospital to fire on the Coalition forces in the CPA compound. For this reason I had decided against sending Fadi there following his release as they were under siege and the outcome of the battle wasn't clear. In response, on 9 April the Coalition forces moved to retake the hospital, the ensuing conflict resulting in considerable structural damage.

What happened next remains contentious. Some Iraqis accused the Americans of intentionally wrecking the hospital once they were in control, supposedly while searching for weapons. The doctors accused the Americans of illegally detaining them during the hospital's first night of liberation/occupation, treating them as if they were militia. The US soldiers conversely claimed that the hospital and all of its equipment was already damaged or stolen before they arrived and that they spent three months cleaning it up.

Regardless of what actually transpired, equipment was looted, the sanitation system destroyed, and windows and doors damaged or stolen. The director of the hospital, Dr Safa al-Ameedi described the situation to my colleagues three weeks after the battle in late April 2004:

'There was a ward-by-ward shooting match with the Spanish-led forces...twenty Iraqis were killed that day along with an American soldier and a Salvadoran...it seems weapons had been stockpiled on the roof of the hospital without my knowledge...there were running battles through the hospital and its operating theatres. Two patients were shot dead as they lay in bed. Two medics were shot dead.'

He described the aftermath as 'amputated limbs in the operating theatres putrefying, blood supplies going to waste,' adding that without action 'water from a leak in the basement would soon contaminate medical supplies, bedding and other materials. No one is overseeing the sewage system.'

However, even as the fighting settled and normality returned, the hospital remained closed.

With a capacity for 1,750 outpatients and 600 beds it was a huge blow to the medical system in the area. Our staff had met with Dr Safa after the fighting. He was told that he couldn't re-open the hospital until the outside doors were repaired to ensure safety from looters, and the water and sanitation system rehabilitated to allow for basic hygiene. We were told that the US had committed twenty-seven million dollars to the hospital, but the money would have to undertake the laborious journey of passing through the Government of Iraq's Ministry of Health—a journey that usually saw far fewer dollars come out than go in. So with existing funding, local staff and in-house expertise, we moved quickly and took responsibility for the water supply system and left the remaining challenges to others.

Walking through the hospital grounds, it was hard to imagine that this had been the centre of a massive military operation. Unlike buildings in other war-ravaged countries such as Bosnia and Herzegovina, where after fifteen years they still bear the marks in part as a reminder of the war or alternatively simply ignored out of neglect, I couldn't see any obvious scars on the Al Sadr hospital.

Waiting to meet with us was Dr Abdulaal Hassan Alghazali, deputy director of the hospital. He was a doctor and an administrator, professions that alone would intimidate most people, but he had decided to combine them and took on the challenge with relish. I admired his dedication. As with most Iraqi working professionals, regardless of the strength of their beliefs, Dr Abdulaal eschewed the traditional Arab garb during the day, dressing in a suit with no tie, only his neatly trimmed beard a sign of his religiosity.

As we sat in the sumptuous couches that so many senior managers in Iraq love to have in their offices, I asked him what role foreign organisations had played in supporting the hospital.

'Many,' he said as Haider translated, 'even if they were small contributions they were crucial to the operation of the hospital.' He paused while staff continued to come and go, bringing paperwork for him to sign and steaming hot tea for us. In Iraq meetings are held in open rooms with people coming and going, often holding parallel conversations, participants multitasking by signing papers or answering phones while continuing to respond to the matter at hand. It's a cultural trait not meant as a personal sleight.

'The support your organisation provided is a good example. The old tanks leaked, loosening the soil and damaging the building. Sometimes we did not have water.' He was referring to the hospital's dilapidated water tanks. 'As a result, the entire system would often shut down, reducing activity in the hospital until water trucks could arrive. What IRC did was crucial. You had also helped repair medical equipment after the first Najaf war,' he reminded us. I had forgotten about this component of our work. We'd repaired equipment including x-ray and ECG machines, plasma refrigerators and defibrillators.

'What about now, where does the Najaf Teaching Hospital stand today?' I asked, considering that tens of millions of dollars had been ploughed into rebuilding the structure and restocking its shelves.

'We need a lot more support,' Dr Abdulaal began, the question seemingly touching a raw nerve. 'The whole of Iraq has only one radiotherapy machine. In India there are fourteen centres. I fly my patients to India for treatment.' Another staff member floated into the room with papers to be signed. I took the opportunity to sip my tea again and consider what he had said, as it was a telling remark. For Iraqis old enough to remember the seventies, such as Dr Abdulaal Hassan, there is a painful understanding of how far the country has fallen. I often sense resentment or despair when talking to these older Iraqis as the conversation inevitably turns to countries where they now travel for medical care or a better quality of life; countries that they previously saw as backwaters relative to their own prosperity.

Judging by the number of people walking in and out of the office, Dr Abdulaal was in high demand and was needed elsewhere so I began to excuse us. 'Thank you for allowing us the time to meet with you. If you don't mind, can we see the water tanks?'

'Of course,' he replied.

On our way out we walked past the four 156,000-litre water tanks IRC had built, still clearly in good order, well maintained, and fully utilised.

* * *

The next day we left Najaf around ten in the morning, heading south to the rural areas straddling the Euphrates River while the air was still cool and the sun not too strong. At one point the wide open desert expanse abruptly gave way to the abundant date palms and thick shrubbery of the river basin. Once enveloped by the lush landscape the temperature dropped markedly. Driving through the vegetation I noticed that the colours weren't the lush green I anticipated from a distance but instead they were dulled, as if diluted. When we passed close to the bushes I could see that sand blown in from the Sea of Najaf had left a thin film of the desert's hue on every leaf and fern, disappointing the eye. Everyone finds their own country uniquely beautiful. To the Iraqis this was paradise, an oasis of vegetation and fresh water, but to me it failed to live up to the anticipation.

Qasem, the agent of Iraq's FBI, decided to come with us as he felt obliged to provide security, though as far as I could see he wasn't carrying any weapons so I wasn't quite sure what he'd do if we were attacked. Nevertheless, along with Haider and Farouq, I felt taken care of.

Our first stop was a village called Barakia where we met Rasool, the maintenance man for the village's water treatment plant, who was milling about as we arrived. He was dressed in a grease-stained white dishdasha with sleeves rolled up ready to repair any breakdown.

Rasool had been hired by the government to monitor and maintain the water treatment plant. Although it was still early in the day the heat was becoming oppressive. As we weaved our way over the pipes and around the valves a gentle breeze carried the thin mist that formed from the constant flow of water and then cooled by the tall reeds growing along the banks. I thought Rasool was the luckiest man in town. I wanted to stay there for the whole day—it was more than pleasant.

'IRC,' he said, pointing at the fence around the plant. 'IRC,' as he touched the chlorine system. He continued by tapping the pump, filter and tank. 'IRC, IRC, IRC'. Rasool had been around since 1998, working on the same water treatment plan. 'After the First Gulf War when maintenance stopped,' he told us as Haider translated, 'there were a lot of diseases in the village. Now it is all good.' Although Rasool wasn't a doctor, I suspected that he knew the health trends in the surrounding villages.

Upstream from Najaf, major cities such as Ramadi and Falluja, each with a population of half a million, discharged untreated sewage into the river. It wasn't until 2004 that work began on Falluja's first sewage treatment plant, but it was never completed, nor had it been completed by Islamic State when they took over Falluja in January of 2014. That evening I read a report about Falluja's sewage treatment plant in which the director of the hospital was quoted as suspecting ten to fifteen per cent of his patients were hospitalised due to 'water or sewage-related diseases'. If this was accurate, Rasool was right; there would have been a marked change after the repairs of his water treatment plant.

While we had jumped in quick and early to rehabilitate all of the forty-eight water treatment plants in the governorate of Najaf, the water department had followed up once it was back on its feet with its own significant and ongoing maintenance program. I wondered, had we not intervened, how long would it have been before the water department did what they were clearly capable of doing themselves? Would it have been a matter of weeks or months or years? Later, I asked some of the former IRC engineers what their thoughts were. One of them, a bright young man called Kaiser Aljid, told me that he had worked as a contractor for the water department after leaving IRC and that most of the maintenance and repair programs were restarted in 2005, with some starting even earlier.

Iraq is not a poor country, and both the hospital and the water department have their own budgets. It seemed that what we had succeeded in doing was simply to jump in early and get the job done quickly. By all accounts the aid to the hospital and water treatment plants was worthwhile, but was this the best way to channel aid—by repairing infrastructure already in disuse for decades in a relatively wealthy country that would be able, within a year or two, to make the repairs themselves using their own funds at a fraction of the cost?

As with most moral dilemmas in the humanitarian world, this line of thought leads to the larger questions of how do we decide which crisis or calamity deserves assistance. In 2000, working as a shelter engineer in East Timor, I was providing emergency housing valued at about five hundred dollars per family. This was a relatively high profile regional crisis. In Sudan, during a long-forgotten war, we could hardly muster financing for forty-dollar shelters. While in the Balkans, at Europe's doorstep, international donors provided housing rehabilitation kits valued in the thousands of dollars. Here in Iraq we were spending millions on rehabilitating water treatment plants and health care facilities that would be fixed by the authorities within a relatively short timeframe anyway. While at about the same time in Darfur (early 2006), where the first genocide of the twenty-first century was already well publicised, the World Food Programme had to cut food aid by half because it could not raise enough funds. The three million Darfuris dependent upon food aid had to survive on a package providing just one thousand and fifty calories per person per day (half of the daily minimum intake required by an adult) because the international community couldn't find the funds.

The inequity is stark and the justification for it weak. It is heartbreaking for aid workers in high profile emergencies to have bottomless budgets for projects and even luxuries for themselves, yet have so few resources when posted to much more pressing, but low-profile crises. As we drove back to Najaf, I decided to ask Haider to try to organise a meeting with the governor of Najaf. I was interested to hear his thoughts on the international community's efforts to rebuild Iraq.

Political campaigning Iraqi style

When I first met Um Ali she was already a widow, a thirty-something young woman whose husband, along with one of her brothers, had died fighting in the Iran-Iraq war. Sadly, fate didn't give her a special pass for already having lost so much. A few years later her second brother was executed by Saddam for avoiding military service. A bill was sent for the cost of the bullet. By the time of the invasion she had lived more than a lifetime's share of sorrow.

I first got to know her in 2003 when she joined the IRC as a health education officer. I saw the flame burning deep inside, though her sorrow was never far from the surface. A mention of her past would bring tears to her eyes. Whereas every woman was expected to dress in black so as not to attract a man's attention, Nawal wore it as if she was in mourning. She was kind enough to have invited me and Kunera, an Arabic-speaking Dutch colleague who was Fadi's predecessor, to her modest house one summer evening. The dinner, served on the floor of an outside courtyard, was generous and sumptuous. We met her children and her second husband, the brother of her deceased husband. She showed me how to weave using a traditional Iraqi wooden loom. She told me her story.

Seven years had passed since we first sat together; this time we were in the IRO offices talking about that first visit to her house and other memories. I was conscious of the role reversal. She was now a prominent local politician, well known and highly regarded by the community. I was unaffiliated and unemployed. Her success hadn't changed her or the way she treated me; she was still engaging and respectful. I also tried not to let my recent cynicism sully her enthusiasm as, along with everyone else, she seemed to hold her time working with the international community in high regard.

I asked her about her work, having heard about her success from mutual friends. Not looking much older, but having noticeably put on the pounds—it seemed every Iraqi had put on weight after the change of regimes—she began by explaining her new role as a member of the Najaf Provincial Council, a sort of state legislature. 'We're responsible for anything related to provincial level issues such as issuing laws, monitoring governmental departments and directorates, the provincial budget, and strategic and urban planning for the province,' she began, with Haider once again translating.

'What have you voted on so far? Any major successes?' I enquired, not knowing much about the Provincial Council. I wasn't sure whether it was just a rubber stamp institution, with puppets appointed by the prominent parties and the inclusion of women such as Nawal simply to meet gender targets imposed by Westerners, or a genuine legislature with active and committed members that included women chosen on their merit. Either way it was an impressive accomplishment for her.

'Regulatory issues mainly, institutional support and urban planning laws,' she answered. As for her biggest achievement to date, it was 'voting on the law of changing Al-Mishkhab area to be a district instead of a suburb.'

'What about your campaign? How do women campaign in Najaf when it's so conservative?' Then I said in jest, 'Do you go door knocking?' I explained the concept knowing full well that this wasn't done in Iraq and certainly not by a woman.

'My campaign was self-financing so I visited friends' houses in addition to using posters,' she told me. Imagine the courage: a woman in one of the most conservative Islamic cities in the world campaigning in a country still at war while death squads intent on destroying democracy and female empowerment roamed the streets.

'I received the highest number of votes among all of the women candidates in Najaf during the elections.' She beamed, holding up her index finger to emphasise that she was first. 'I am so proud of that because I have my people's support and trust, hence, I will keep serving them as much as I can towards better life and better society.'

Unlike most women in Najaf, Nawal was forthright with her opinions and unashamed to express her feelings openly. But a whole life living in a culture that separated the roles of men and women couldn't be washed away with a new title and political responsibility. Her lips were always slightly curled as she spoke, primed to stretch out into a smile to lighten her seriousness or soften her opinions and even ready to break into laughter as if to say, 'That's my opinion, but I'm just a woman.'

'Does being a woman in a rigid patriarchy negatively affect your ability to be an effective member of the Council?' I asked.

'On the contrary, it helps me a lot as people respect my achievements for this and appreciate my work towards serving the society regardless of my gender.'

'What are you currently working on in the Council?' I asked.

'Now we're participating in monitoring the government departments in our province and also working on the provincial budget,' she went on. At this point we paused as some rice and boiled meat was brought in.

'Okay, I know you well enough that you must be fighting for something. What are you fighting for?' I prodded.

This brought a spark to her face. 'I am now working with some lawyers to put together legislation regarding women's rights since the government in Baghdad is not open to the idea of women holding senior positions in ministries, and the same thing is happening here at the level of Provincial Council. I will try to do my best and work on giving women on the Provincial Council a bigger share of power through changing the distribution of the current committees. This is my first priority now—working on issuing this legislation.' She turned to face me squarely, looking me in the eye as she got to the heart of the matter: 'I am the only woman who stands up for women. Seven other women [on the council], they are quiet and passive.' At this point Nawal mimicked them by making a face of submission and slouching back. Sitting once again firmly in her chair, she went on. 'They have no experience and no interest to fight the men for important issues.' She spoke forcefully, yet I could see her lips curled again, ready to roll out into that knowing smile.

'Just one year ago,' Nawal continued, holding up her index finger to make sure the translation didn't go astray, 'Najaf government hired women police to work on the streets. Only last year! Health education is also important. International organisations should work more to teach the people about good health.'

A couple of others at the table joked that men were afraid of her. I could believe it as she hadn't lost her forthrightness. But I knew in most cases their fear would have been of her breaching cultural etiquette rather than an acknowledgement of her superior mind or better argument.

Slipping back into my role of interviewer, seeking out the past, I asked Nawal about her memories of the time she spent working with us. 'Very good memories. Kunera and Dijana were like sisters, inspiring me to achieve,' she said of the two female expatriates with whom she had worked. Nawal's raw strength as a woman playing for a tough crowd reminded me of Dijana, whose journey to Iraq was inspiring to all who learned of her story. Still in high school when the war broke out in the Balkans, Dijana had joined an aid agency associated with the Knights of Malta and worked hard in Bosnia and Herzegovina, Albania and her own country, Croatia. By the time the United States invaded Iraq, Dijana had worked her way up through the ranks as a local staff member and was selected by the IRC for their first response team as a team leader. Initially based in Amman, she waited out the invasion along with the rest of the team and then crossed into Iraq only weeks after the fall of Baghdad with $10,000 in cash spread amongst her various undergarments to be used to establish operations.

I first met Dijana in Baghdad in 2003 when I was the head of the Najaf office and travelled to the capital for meetings. It was a balmy evening; we'd all finished our team meetings and decided to have a few beers in the garden of our small hotel. Random gunfire, tank treads tearing at the tarmac, and helicopters buzzing overhead drowned out the music. Peter, the dancing photographer, was there as were other expatriates from across the country, including, from memory, Biserka, a hard smoking and heavy drinking Macedonian water and sanitation specialist. Dijana and Biserka were good friends and both being from the Balkans spent considerable time speaking in their own language. I pretended that I didn't understand and my friends who knew that I could speak it fluently played coy. It was cheating—I would flirt a little with Dijana and then listen to the gossip between the two, adjust my game and then feign disinterest while listening covertly again. We continued like that for most of the night before I could no longer hold back, laughing and telling them that I could understand every word they said.

At least that's how I remembered it, though Dijana, now my wife, insists the conversations with Biserka were over the phone and that I wasn't very good at flirting.

As a woman, Dijana had access to a part of Iraqi society that was closed to male aid workers, regardless of whether they were Iraqi or foreigners. To achieve success in her role she required a unique set of skills and a willingness to embrace the culture and its discriminatory etiquette. On many occasions when we visited officials or attended functions, my male colleagues and I would walk through the main entrance of a house and meet with the purported decision makers and leaders, who were all men, while

Dijana would meet with the women. The conversations were different, but of equal importance. Whereas I learned of the power structures and economic circumstances, Dijana would hear a more grounded view of the people's needs. She would learn of the challenges families were facing, the hardships of different groups in society, and the immediate needs to which we could respond without the political opportunism that would taint much of the advice I would hear.

Having imposed clothing guidelines for both men (no shorts despite the heat) and women (a hijab) while visiting conservative areas of Iraq, I was of the view that we had to focus on life-saving priorities and accept the cultural context of the community. We were guests in a society whose cultural norms were theirs to change and not for us to impose change. Despite my regressive views, Dijana never complained. I admired Dijana for her drive just as I admired Nawal for hers.

Nawal continued recalling her memories of working with us: 'With the IRC I learned practical skills such as public speaking, using a computer, and project management. Most importantly, I saw dedication to work, and commitment, working with rules instead of the chaos that Iraqis work in.'

Although I had little to lay claim to, as Kunera and Dijana clearly helped Nawal find this new path, nevertheless I felt proud of her success.

'I am now studying political science, one more year,' Nawal announced, again raising her index finger. Another surprise that added to my admiration.

'Do you plan on running for higher political office, for a more senior position?' I asked, hopeful that she would.

'Yes, of course. It is my dream and I will keep working to make it happen,' she said with confidence.

Her name in Arabic means 'gift'. I think that she truly is a gift to the Iraqi people.

As the time neared for us to move to the meeting with the

governor, Nawal asked if she could come along as she hadn't seen him for a while and had a few things to tell him. I acquiesced but asked her to refrain from saying anything until after our meeting, only half joking that she might put his nose out of joint prior to our conversation.

Gifts for the governor

As we left the car and walked up to the governor's offices, I counted five American MRAPs. These beasts on wheels are Mine Resistant Ambush Protected vehicles, resembling lunar-landing pods with antennas galore and other strange contraptions protruding from every side. I walked by trying my best not to wave at the soldiers holed up inside.

It was a Saturday, a day off for government workers, so we strolled around the long corridors, shuttling from one waiting room to another. The few people there—guards, receptionists, and personal assistants—seemed surprised to see a Westerner without security. The guards at the entrance didn't know what to make of the situation. They looked down at my Australian passport, glanced around the room to spot my security detail, not finding any looked down again to confirm that I was a Westerner, and looked up again to search more thoroughly for the burly guards that always accompanied foreigners.

'Welcome,' was all I got in return.

On several other occasions, guards would read my passport upside down or acknowledge my identification based upon a generic membership card I thrust their way. This was never a good sign.

Once we were escorted in, there were profuse apologies as we were told that the governor was delayed opening a new school, the first in the region for high-performing children. I didn't mind, I felt quite safe in the building. To while away the time I people-watched. Flares seemed to be back in among the young, while Haider's oversized suits were the trend with older men. The few women that were there weren't covered from head to toe in black; instead they wore a hijab and modest, loose-fitting Western clothes. It seemed the governor's offices were a haven for those with slightly more liberal values.

We were moved once more, this time to the VIP visitors' room in a separate building. As none of us had been there before, we childishly made the most of the opportunity and posed regally in the ornate gold-gilded, high-backed chairs, taking photos of each other. This wore thin after a while, so we returned to drinking tea and lounging about reminiscing.

Suddenly, the double doors burst open and a stream of men rushed forward. Haider nodded toward the man dressed immaculately in a dark suit and navy blue tie leading the procession and whispered loudly, 'This is the governor.' Never having seen him before I appreciated the heads-up. The governor, Adnan Zurfi, motioned for me to sit beside him on one of the two head chairs in which we had earlier role-played.

He had to be the only Iraqi I had seen who didn't wear gold. His watch was a heavy stainless steel piece. He wore a ring, but it looked like silver or platinum. There was no other jewellery on him. I was immediately left with the impression that he was different. Being an American citizen and having lived in the United States, he had fluent English skills, so I looked forward to a fluid discussion.

After the pleasantries, I opened with a leading question: 'Do you see a positive role for foreign aid organisations?'

'Since I've been governor I haven't seen many charities come to work in Najaf,' Adnan began. 'International aid organisations are a new idea to Iraq. The political culture is that the government is the only one to provide services. This is partly the government's fault as they see organisations as opponents or competitors. Foreign organisations have a role to play. In today's Iraq we need them to work with the people to educate them on how to be good citizens and demand services from the government the right way.'

This was music to my ears, a perspective on development close to my heart and one that I rarely heard. Zurfi seemed to understand that it was just as important to balance the supply of democracy and government services with the people's ability and willingness to demand it. Creating a robust state structure must be counterbalanced by a robust civil society. Too much of the former leads to autocracy, while an imbalance in favour of the latter to anarchy. Yet the overwhelming effort undertaken by the international community has been towards re-establishing the state without much concern given to civil society. This was particularly interesting considering that during the invasion and subsequent years the United States and Australia both had centre-right governments whose political philosophies were built on smaller government and greater power to the people.

Turning the tables, Adnan asked me, 'What do you think could be an impediment to Iraqi civil society?'

Having thought about this often, I was ready with an answer. 'I don't see volunteerism flourishing. There is no broad sense of community and the responsibilities that come with that in Iraq. People seem to be focused on themselves and their families surviving, or their clan and their tribe prospering, but not so willing to help strangers. Yet a sense of community beyond blood relatives is a critical component of functioning societies.'

Volunteering is a powerful mechanism through which solidarity can be built. It helps people reach across social divisions and hierarchies to develop empathy for the other, in such a way that Christians get to know Muslims, CEOs rub shoulders with the homeless, and migrants and long-standing residents learn from each other. This type of volunteering is important for societies to bridge the chasms that are built over time and even more so those that are created from wars when societies tend to fracture into isolated groups.

He corrected me on this point.

'Iraqis are a very generous people. Many thousands of widows of the wars were secretly supported by Iraqis voluntarily during Saddam's time. The problem is that the government doesn't have a system to encourage the creation of local NGOs.' He gave me an example: contractors bidding for work from the Najaf government often want to give a 'gift' to the government, and he tells them to donate to a local charity or a religious group; of course, they don't as it defeats the initial intent of the 'gift' and there is no other reason to give. 'In the United States donations get tax deductions. Not here.'

'I hope to create an incentive system for giving,' Adnan continued, with a note of optimism in his voice. I liked his long-term vision. I had met government officials in Hilla, a neighbouring governorate, only a few years earlier who were only focused on the short term. When allocating funds, one department decided to pave the footpaths as they wanted people to see change. It didn't seem to matter to them that the same footpaths were being dug up immediately after by another department responsible for the water and sewage networks, which also wanted people to see change.

The governor continued, 'There are two types of local organisations. Those that truly believe in democracy, such as IRO,' he said, motioning towards Haider, 'and there are those set up for personal benefit or by political parties. These are bound to fail.'

'Do you have a preference for the type of foreign aid organisation providing the aid, such as the United Nations, for-profit contractors, Provincial Reconstruction Teams, or NGOs?' I asked, wondering where the governor stood on the same question I had asked the Ayatollah.

'All aid is the same, it doesn't matter what the vehicle is. Though, when we're talking about community development, the local groups are better suited; but for specialist technical support, the foreign organisations are welcome.'

After some casual chatter, I sensed it was time to wrap up. As we walked out from the room the governor drew Haider aside and asked him about Fadi. Haider, like me, didn't have any news and politely responded that he was well. I had missed this connection. Adnan had been installed by the Americans as Najaf's newly minted governor on 10 April 2004, four days after Fadi had been kidnapped. The previous governor had simply fled, leaving his post and all his responsibilities.

Haider told me afterwards that Adnan was still sorry for the situation and emphasised that he had done his best to help Fadi. I was once again reminded of how many people came out to support Fadi. Clearly the people of Najaf had heeded the parable of Imam Ali escorting the Christian home.

Walking away from this meeting I couldn't help but like the governor. He was sharp, open in his answers, and saw the challenges facing Iraqi civil society far beyond his own immediate political ambitions. I told Haider and Nawal that if I could, I would vote for him.

The next day I flew out of Iraq. It was great to catch up with old friends, but unsurprisingly the journey had only led to more questions than answers. I left trying to make sense of the interviews to when I was safely home, until then I just savoured the memories of the visit.

Ghost soldiers

As I returned home from Iraq I reflected on what I'd seen. It was clear that most of the aid projects initiated and implemented during the first few years in Iraq were only band-aid measures. It's no surprise then that with hindsight it appears as if the aid operation in Iraq was more a marketing mission focused at showing results—I'm still not quite sure to whom, Washington or the Iraqis—at the expense of long-term sustainable development. Money became an end in itself rather than a means to an end. Our performance was measured against our ability to spend. This led to big ticket 'emergency' projects even though there was no emergency to speak of. Projects such as rehabilitating the hospital or the water treatment plants were our only options as our funding was restricted by the donor to three- and six-month projects. Our objective was to reach as many beneficiaries as possible in a time period that defied logic. One not-for-profit group was found to have reported their projects as reaching numbers far exceeding the entire population of Iraq.

The 'emergency' that we were funded to respond to in reality was cosmetic; we were in a hurry to improve the image of the Coalition forces. But the problem was that by tying charities to the actions of the military, the actions of the military would be tied to the work of charities. Ostracised by the civilian population, targeted by terrorists or, as in my case, looked upon suspiciously by religious leaders such as the Ayatollah, charities were and continue to be faced with the 'damned if you do, damned if you don't' dilemma of choosing sides.

But despite these challenges and their accompanying failures there was one element of our past activities that made me proud—our staff. They had gone from strength to strength, with ideals and values that were given impetus through their time working alongside us. Nawal's fight for women's rights and Haider and Firas' civil society organisation are just two examples of the new Iraq in which the Iraqis themselves are pushing for change but within their own cultural parameters and at their own pace. We gave them the means to fight their own fight, an approach that is much more sustainable and successful than imposing solutions and demanding that they follow through with them. Not that this wasn't tried: USAID attempted to create a civil society in sixteen months immediately following the invasion by tendering a $43 million contract for that purpose. Not surprisingly it failed. Alongside this attempted quick fix were other efforts such as assisting with the writing of legislation that was thought would automatically lead to reform, the running of elections that were presumed would lead to democracy, or the training of women that was aimed at rebalancing gender roles. Change develops organically. It needs credible local champions to lead movements at a pace and in a way that pushes the cultural boundaries without breaking them.

A few weeks after I flew out of Najaf, Haider got the call to pack his bags for a new life in the United States. Firas had been placed in Mobile, Alabama, and I had joked with Haider that he'd be sent to Anchorage, Alaska. Instead he was off to California.

I tried to connect Nawal with a few organisations involved in democracy building as she had asked for help in accessing additional training and building networks to international women's groups. One of them, the National Democratic Institute, promised to add her to their list once they received her resume. But it seemed fate was not yet done with her family. In December one of her brothers was involved in a car accident that left him paralysed.

Nawal asked if I could get a second opinion from outside doctors, but both Jordanian specialists to whom I sent the reports and MRI scans confirmed that nothing more could be done.

Qasem, of the Iraqi FBI, had asked me to try to get his son a scholarship to study abroad. His son had been accepted into the prestigious school of dentistry in Falluja, a Sunni stronghold, which basically barred him, a Shia, from studying with any sense of safety. Another reminder that Iraq still had a long way to go before its people could live normal lives.

A few months later the Arab Spring roared through the Middle East. Beginning in December 2010 with a street seller angry at the heavy handedness of the Tunisian police, it spread to Syria, Egypt, and Libya. Iraq seemed untouched, with the former US officials involved in the early days of the Iraq saga claiming that the region's new-found enthusiasm for democracy was a result of the democratic seed planted in Iraq. This reading of events was overly enthusiastic if not naïve. Iraq was not free from the democratic fervour; it simply didn't play out as many had thought. Rather than Iraq being a beacon of light shining into the darker despotic corners of the Middle East, the democratic experience upturned the status quo with a newly empowered, numerically superior Shia dominating elections and in turn government. In a country shaped by tribal and religious identity, democracy had legitimated the rule of the majority with no protections for the minority. Endemic corruption exacerbated the problems by facilitating the emergence of a ruling elite who acquired power through familial relations or religious affiliation.

The losers from this change of political system were the Sunnis. Saddam had favoured Sunni leaders as had the British before. From these positions of privilege, the fall felt especially hard. Tariq al-Hashimi, Iraq's one-time Vice President, called the Sunni uprisings in Iraq against the democratically elected government their Arab Spring, a twist to the popular Western conception of the oppressor who in his eyes was the democratically elected government.

For the international community, the more than $200 billion of Iraqi and US money that was spent on rebuilding the country appeared lost. Corruption had become so entrenched that even senior officers in the Iraqi armed forces were forced to buy their ranks. The debt was paid by adding names to payroll, in effect creating ghost soldiers. When Islamic State swept across the border into Iraq, the thousands of ghost soldiers were no match for the few hundred fanatics. Within a year, the group controlled a third of Iraq including the second largest city, Mosul, and the capital of Anbar province, Ramadi. Islamic State's appeal to the people was to revert their lives to a much simpler and purer time, a time when Islamic culture dominated the region. Although their rule in Iraq didn't last beyond 2017, the impact on society will last generations. Will the Sunnis be trusted by the people and the government again? Can the Shia put aside their historical animosity and find a path towards peace for all Iraqis?

Dijana with the chief of security, Salar, in the foreground and a guard in the background

No Dancing, No Dancing ~ 151

The author with Haider with the Shrine of Imam Ali in the background

The author with Ayatollah Sheikh Bashir

Speaking with Dr Abdulaal Hassan Alghazali at the Najaf Teaching Hospital

Waiting for the governor with Nawal in the background

PART THREE
East Timor

Kumbaya

Flying from Darwin to East Timor's capital Dili across the Timor Sea on an Embraer 170, all I could think about was a burly man from Kentucky. Admittedly, it's a strange thought on a journey to a former Portuguese colony that was annexed by Indonesia, liberated by an Australian-led multinational force and with its only tie to the United States being the official currency.

That man from Kentucky was Brian Walker. He took over the role of country director for the International Rescue Committee around the time I arrived in May 2000. Larger than life in so many ways, he cut an imposing figure amongst the smaller Timorese people, taller than my six foot two and much bulkier. He was an aid worker cut from a mould all too rare these days—he served in the roughest of neighbourhoods for years at a time when air-conditioned houses, internet, and satellite phones were only found in the homes of dictators and money launderers, not aid workers. Old school by nature, he didn't give a damn about his career, invariably siding with the Timorese above headquarters, the rest of the international community or even the law. Also, less admirably, old school in his management style, he was prone to shouting, dismissing others' ideas, and staying clear of anything smelling of bureaucracy. Despite these flaws, I admired him.

East Timor appeared on Brian's radar in 1999, as with much of the rest of the world, when a vote on the future of Indonesia's twenty-seventh province was organised by the United Nations.

After twenty-five years of Indonesian annexation, this former Portuguese colony went to the polls to vote for or against autonomy with Indonesia, and 98.6% of the eligible population did, knowing a vote against autonomy was acknowledged by all parties, including Indonesia, as an implicit vote for independence. People quietly went to vote on 30 August 1999, returning home not to celebrate but to pack up their belongings, leaving their homes before the day ended knowing full well what lay ahead. Over the following days and weeks an estimated quarter of the entire population, approximately two hundred thousand people seeking safety, fled across the land border into neighbouring West Timor, a province of Indonesia. Many others took to the mountains where the Timorese resistance still held control. Militias loyal to Indonesian power-brokers laid waste to the towns, resulting in complete devastation. Few houses anywhere were left standing while many areas ended up looking like war zones. Using technology from a bygone era—machetes, torches and brute force—a relatively small group of militias destroyed an entire country.

Following the violence the international community responded quickly. Led by Australian troops, an international force landed in East Timor on 16 September 1999. Administration of the devastated country was handed over to an international body called the United Nations Transitional Administration in East Timor (UNTAET) in October of the same year. For the first time the United Nations became a sovereign authority. Thousands of international bureaucrats were hired from all over the world to fill posts in an interim government. The new head of state was the Brazilian diplomat, Sergio Vieira de Mello, who subsequently died in a massive truck bomb in Iraq. His death in Iraq was claimed by al-Qaeda, who accused him of being a 'crusader' responsible for extracting 'a part of the Islamic land', East Timor, from Islam. I was in Najaf when he along with twenty-one others died in the massive explosion at the United Nations headquarters in Baghdad. His deputy in East Timor was from the Philippines. Security contingents were sent from Asia, the Middle East, South America, Africa, Australia, and Europe. It became the Island of Babel, with not only different languages creating confusion but also varying work ethics, cultures, policies and procedures, mandates and missions.

Among this wave of newcomers were hundreds of NGOs and development agencies—some working under the auspices of UN agencies, others not—each with their own urgent agenda, primacy of purpose, and certainty of success. Brian headed one such agency, leading a team of about a dozen expatriates and nearly a hundred Timorese. I arrived during the first days of May 2000, taking up my first aid posting as a shelter engineer.

Despite his appearance, Brian brought a 'kumbaya' tone to the organisation, which only served to strengthen my belief in our ability to remake East Timor into a safe, stable, and prosperous country. This first posting was exactly what I had imagined an aid mission would be—we lived in a sparsely furnished former convent with intermittent electricity, and no hot water or air conditioning. Our beds were mattresses on the floor with mosquito nets draped above to prevent being infected with malaria or dengue. A lunch of steamed rice and vegetables was provided as there weren't any restaurants or supermarkets. The jungle reached all the way to the city's main streets where cocks crowed in the mornings, water buffaloes roamed along the streets, pigs sniffed through the rubbish, and wise-looking goats wandered freely. Tasked with distributing emergency shelter kits, we visited idyllic hillside villages by car or on foot, meeting each home owner to determine eligibility for our program. Despite returning home each day exhausted and wet from the humidity and sweat, I felt we were making a positive change at the grass-roots level.

The IQ of a Dog

After a few months I started to question some of the actions of the more 'august' organisations. Together with a few of my East Timorese friends I went to the local newspaper and applied to take out a quarter-page advertisement. This wasn't something the newspaper was used to as most adverts were for businesses and my intentions were clearly different. I persisted, bringing up freedom of the press, independence, liberty, and any other popular political catchphrase I could think of before they eventually agreed, money changed hands, and my idea took shape. When the edition hit the stands the following week, readers flicking through the pages found details of the newly minted 'UNdeserving Award'. In its inaugural form it was awarded to Johannes Wortel, Director for Administration, for 'his recent decree that all NGOs are not allowed to access the internet in UNTAET field offices.' Despite this, he continued to allow a for-profit travel agency that organised UN staff holidays to access their network along with giving UN staff and peacekeepers unrestricted usage that included porn, games, and running their side businesses. However, aid workers based in the devastated countryside could not use the same network to send reports or updates to Dili, or write home to their families.

A Yahoo email address accompanied the award inviting others to send their nominations. There were a lot of contenders for the next award. Should it go to the UN official who decided to impose a tax on goods while allowing UN staff to access the same goods tax free? Or maybe to the UN staff member who chose to fly frozen fish in from Sydney to stock their kitchens while cutting back on programs to help the Timorese because of a shortage of funds. Or maybe to whoever decided to rent a cruise ship at US$6 million per month to house UN staff for over a year rather than rebuild the devastated capital and leave something behind when they left. I received a deluge of other submissions but I left it at that. I didn't want to create too much controversy. That is, until one evening I went to a friend's going away dinner.

Having just come back from a trip into the countryside in mid-December, I was looking forward to an evening out in the new, re-energised, cosmopolitan Dili. The crowd at the dinner was mainly from the United Nation's transitional government, people from all over the world, responsible for the Dili district. The girl on her way out was Italian, while those seated near my end of the table were from the United States, Kosovo, and Norway. Drinks were bought, food ordered, and the conversation rolled along easily. One of the Americans somehow got to the topic of the four air-conditioning units in her house. From there the rest of the evening's conversation began to deteriorate.

'Why would you need four air-conditioners? The electricity company is already running at full throttle, preventing any new connections. For every air-conditioner you're running, that's at least one Timorese family without lighting in their home,' I blustered despite being the newbie aid worker.

The response was quick and sharp: 'I don't care.'

The Kosovar, a human rights officer, chimed in, 'They're out on the streets till five am anyway. That's why they don't work.'

The other American in the room added, 'They don't need electricity because they don't read. That's why they have an IQ of a dog.'

'Anyway, they don't wash, so why would they need electricity?' the four air-conditioners American added.

I remember saying to the human rights officer, 'You should be ashamed for referring to East Timorese that way,' but coming from a twenty-six-year-old first timer it didn't hit the mark.

Too early in the night to attribute his crassness to alcohol, he unabashedly continued, 'My dog is better, at least it can be trained.'

The arguments continued to and fro, with each round more heated. I pointed out that half of our organisation's expatriate staff had handed over responsibilities to Timorese staff that now ran multi-million dollar projects. We had sent staff to Spain, Jakarta, and Darwin for training, empowered them with authority, and provided guidance on international standards while allowing them to run with day-to-day operations. 'That's why they're probably still working in the office while I'm here drinking it up with you guys,' I said, though I should have said 'you idiots'.

Our host joined me in trying to rebut some of the nasty, racist, and completely nonsensical ideas being expressed. But I couldn't take it anymore, nor did I want to spend more time with such people. For the first time in my life I got up from a dinner, excused myself and left. This wasn't development; it was the worst of colonialism all over again.

The next day I talked my experience over with Brian and he encouraged me to write to a newspaper. A few weeks later my opinion piece appeared in major newspapers in Australia precipitating an intimidating call from the United Nations Secretary-General's office in New York, along with being ostracised from social events in Dili. More importantly it led to the establishment of a Board of Inquiry, though I never learned what came of it. I suspect nothing much.

Four languages, one country

Preparing for my trip back I began reading through articles and reports covering the time I was there. While I made my voice heard through the UNdeserving Awards and the opinion piece, others with more credibility and a much longer commitment to East Timor were as well. Recalling these episodes as I was returning, I tried to relate it to my recent visits to South Sudan and Iraq where people like Matthew, Peter, and Nawal emphasised an important message—it's the people, stupid. It seems that there is something very wrong when people are paid substantial salaries, placed in positions of responsibility with absolute authority, yet have complete disrespect or even disdain for the people they are paid to serve. For example, one 'aid worker' that I read about, Gerald Gahima, left Rwanda in 2004 under a cloud of questions about personal debts and allegations of misuse of office as a judge. Yet four years later he was made 'senior justice adviser' to East Timor on a two-year $757,960 tax free contract (*Herald Sun*, 23 May 2010).

Before taking to the road and heading into the Timorese countryside to see what happened to the projects I was involved in, I wanted to get a sense of the political events that were transpiring around me while we were lugging wooden planks and roof sheeting around the country. This was the first time the international aid community had run a country, and considering the decades of experience each UN bureaucrat brought, did they do any better?

I went to meet Dr Louis da Costa in his offices at the Universitas de Pas. It took some time to find the campus as the taxi driver hadn't been there before. Once we were in the general area we were guided through a series of back streets by locals who pointed us along rocky dirt roads through a semi-rural area that I doubted would lead to one of this country's major universities with over three thousand students, but it did. Ending in a clearing we parked under a tree among several recently built two-storey structures.

During my first stint in East Timor I hadn't heard of Louis, but a few repeated references on the internet to an open letter he had penned piqued my interest. As he was the rector of one of only two internationally accredited universities in East Timor, a Member of Parliament, the head of the parliamentary sub-committee on the economy and a lecturer, I really didn't expect to be given much of his time. Fortunately, my presumption was incorrect.

Like so many other Timorese he had few worry lines etched across his face even though clearly Louis, along with his compatriots, had lived through so much. Only a receding hairline and a slow gait gave his age away. We sat down in a large white tiled and white walled room on the second floor of the main campus building. On the architectural drawings I suspect that this space would have been labelled as a conference room or executive office, but all we found were three ornately carved wooden framed couches and a coffee table. Our voices echoed against the bare walls.

Not having read the open letter, as it wasn't available online or anywhere else I could get a copy, I presumed that he was a stern critic of the United Nations. 'You were an early fighter for the Timorese voice during the UNTAET time. Was there a moment early in 2000 when you said, I have to stand up, I have to say something about what is happening under UNTAET?' I asked, expecting to record this former senior member of the Timorese resistance slam the same people who years ago I had shown so little regard for.

* * *

The United Nations' role in East Timor, known as Timor-Leste in Portuguese, was a combination of sovereign rule and humanitarian assistance. In a rare show of agility the international community established a stand-alone structure, United Nations Transitional Administration in East Timor (UNTAET), in October 1999 without an existing structure, headquarters or personnel.

It was mandated to be international, a modern day Tower of Babel—twenty-nine countries contributed troops, thirty-nine sent police along with a menagerie of bureaucrats from all corners of the world.

Then it was tasked with a long list of responsibilities including to maintain law and order, establish an effective administration, assist in the development of civil and social services, coordinate and deliver humanitarian assistance, support capacity-building for self-government, and establish conditions for sustainable development. For good measure, it was given sovereignty four months after the Security Council authorised its establishment and had only two years to operate before having to hand over to local authorities.

At a cost of $477 million, it pales into comparison with recent efforts in Iraq and Afghanistan. Nevertheless, the size of the new country with less than a million people made the effort on a per capita basis a considerable investment in post-conflict state building.

On 30 August 2001 the East Timorese went to the polls to elect an 88-member Constituent Assembly tasked with writing and adopting a new Constitution. East Timor's Constituent Assembly signed a new Constitution on 22 March 2002 and following presidential elections on 14 April, Xanana Gusmao was appointed president-elect of East Timor.

* * *

Sitting in the grand chair that enveloped him he began in his self-taught, hesitant but clear English.

'At the time the transitional period for UNTAET was very short. It was established in 2000 and it was determined that by 2002 it had to hand over governance responsibilities. Because of that it was just a rush of filling the UNTAET bureaucracy with people coming from various countries but without good knowledge of Timor-Leste.' He continued to explain that subsequently, as the UN began to pack their bags and leave, 'UNTAET had to inform the international community that the United Nations mission here was very successful and that was not true. That was why I wrote a letter to the Secretary-General of the United Nations.'

'When you say it was too short, what were your expectations?' I asked.

'At least I expected a transitional period that lasted five years,' he responded.

'It seems to me that you are saying that the people who came were part of the problem, but if it was five years then there would be more people who didn't know about East Timor.'

'Yes, but at least we would have time to select the right people to come to East Timor.'

We got talking about the international community's contribution, the good, the bad, the ugly, and the outright stupid.

'For any project you have in mind to be successfully implemented it has to enjoy the support of the beneficiary,' Louis said. 'People will not support your project if that project, the design of the project, or the process of the project doesn't fit with cultural expectations and needs. It's possible to just solve some short-term need, but after a year you come back and your project is not here anymore. This is why every project has to be based on research including the cultural basis of the community.'

'Was that done here?' I asked.

'Some, but others...' and then he clicked his fingers rapidly to indicate that they just came and went without any impact.

It wasn't necessarily knowing the small cultural nuances, such as when passing between two people deep in conversation that you bend low with one hand dipping down to the ground, but rather paying respect to the expertise that was inherent to being born and raised in a country. The experts too often thought that what works in Bolivia will work in East Timor. In the following days I met with a World Bank specialist who told me that he'd rather hire an expatriate with the right teaching skills and train them up on the technical expertise than a technical expert without the teaching skills. Yet our aid programs are skewed towards recognising experts in obscure fields who have little to no skills in communicating their knowledge in cross-cultural contexts.

'Another problem, our problem,' he told me, 'is that in an interaction between a Timorese and an expatriate, the Timorese has a big barrier, he is thinking in Bahasa Indonesia, but he has to translate into Portuguese because it is our official language, and then speak in English to the international expert. You can imagine a minister or a director spends more time going to the dictionary to find the right meaning of a Portuguese word than actually communicating.'

Memories of this mess were coming back to me. During the period of UN administration there were four working languages—Portuguese, English, Bahasa Indonesian and Tetum, the indigenous language. In the current Constitution, the official languages are identified as Tetum and Portuguese, with English and Bahasa as working languages.

I asked Louis how they had come to this worst of all worlds situation of four languages.

'At the end of 1999 when we were based in Darwin, Xanana Gusmao wanted a discussion on the language. There was a vivid debate between us. I was one of those who argued that English and Bahasa Indonesia were the proper languages as the national languages, while Xanana was of the opinion that Portuguese should be the language because of the cultural ties. We had at that time about three thousand Timorese with bachelor degrees from Indonesia and none from Portugal.'

I said, 'I have heard of younger members of the leadership who walk out of meetings when the older leaders start speaking Portuguese.' This was something Osorio, a fellow former IRC staffer, had told me. Louis nodded in agreement with a smile reaching across his face as if I had discovered a secret.

It was the persistent challenge. The old guard who fought for independence wanted to retain their positions while the youth—the future of the country—wanted the pragmatic option that would allow them to forge ahead with their lives. How different was this to the warlords in South Sudan, who were great warriors but poor bureaucrats yet they held onto positions of control despite the damage they were doing to the country that they professed to love. Were the Iraqi Shia leaders any different by being focused on the past and not willing to comprise by finding a place for the Sunnis?

Dangerous times

Not long after settling into a Chinese-run hotel in Dili, I was eager to get out into the countryside. Dili isn't a big city, rather it's better described as a town. With a population of 150,000 people, it's not overly crowded unless you count the animals that share the roads and paths. My hotel was two streets away from the beach and a short walk away from Castaways, a restaurant and bar that takes up the entire second floor of the wooden, open-air structure with a front row panoramic view of the islands of Atauro, where a small community of Timorese remained untouched by the violence that had gripped the mainland. The restaurant is a metaphor for the juxtaposition of the old East Timor with the new. Pictures of Che Guevara hang on the wall, a relic of the resistance movement's communist roots; Bob Marley's words reverberate with lines that could have been written for the Timorese, 'I'll take you to a land of liberty; Where we can live—live a good, good life; And be free.' Yet, amongst these relics of a bygone era are a new class of Timorese who mingle with oil and gas capitalists, World Bank specialists, and adventure tourists drinking fine wines and expensive cocktails. The revolutionary dreams of the old are being swamped by the new realities of the young with tensions and frustrations emerging. The young bristled when the old guard chose Portuguese as a national language, while the old resented the indifference to the sacrifices they made fighting for the cause. The young want open relations with Indonesia to allow them job opportunities and training; the old distrust their former enemies and instead seek to build ties with other countries.

As relaxing as it was to jog along the waterfront and enjoy the laid-back lifestyle of Castaways where I met with some of my former staff, I was eager to get out into the countryside. It wasn't until the third day that I had organised everything including renting a car, arranging an itinerary, and finding the phone numbers of a few friends that I could meet.

Osorio, my travel companion for the next few days, is my age. Only a few weeks before I arrived he was still working as an adviser to the Minister of Tourism, Commerce and Industry. It was a stressful job that was affecting his health, so he'd decided to take some time off and join me on my journey.

Osorio and I had both studied engineering, joined IRC very early in our careers, and took to our jobs with a lot of energy but with equally sparse experience. Neither of us really knew what we were doing during those early days. After a few months, I spoke with Brian about promoting Osorio to be my deputy and for the remainder of my time in East Timor I slowly handed over responsibilities to him. The job wasn't technically challenging but it was potentially explosive. Of all the humanitarian programs in East Timor, shelter distribution was the most lucrative to some and desperately needed by many. More than seventy per cent of homes had been destroyed during the few months of post-referendum mayhem, and the first rainy season passed while the international aid community was still organising itself and the second was quickly approaching, leaving people exposed to the elements. Our job was to visit the villages and meet with the chiefs as well as holding community meetings where we would announce the qualifying criteria for receiving shelter materials. Some villages were only accessible by foot, requiring long walks along mountain paths while others were just off a main road. A few would put on a warm welcome with a tour and some palm wine and sweet bananas while others were more clinical, focused on the nuts and bolts of the transaction.

At some, I was truly inspired. In Aldeia Terminal a man moved towards the microphone to ask us a question. It wasn't a memorable question, so the community responded by laughing to which he retorted, 'I am just exercising my right to speak in a democracy, we live in a democracy, right?' For the first time in his life he could say that and he was enjoying every moment of his newfound freedom. Or when we had a security situation in one location and the international police were called in to help calm the situation. Along with the foreign faces in their varied uniforms was a Timorese police officer. With surprise and glee, the people were asking, 'Timorese polisia?' He managed to solve the problem simply through his presence. People were not familiar with the authorities being their own people.

It was mid-afternoon as Osorio and I set off, passing the outskirts of Dili where the Pakistani military had been based, past the old port with a few wooden ships docked, and then on to the narrow and winding road that hugs the coastline. Small wooden canoes with outriggers were scouring the sea searching for their day's catch, produce was sold by the pile rather than weight from bamboo stalls on the side of the road, children played in puddles, and water buffalo roamed freely across the fields and roads.

'Isn't it terrible what happened to Brian?' I said to Osorio.

Brian had survived Afghanistan during the devastating civil war, even after someone rolled a hand grenade into the place where he was dining—seeing it happen he managed to save himself by jumping behind the counter. It was a dangerous location for aid workers trying to serve people already battered by nearly two decades of war. Yet he survived, only to be murdered at his Kentucky home along with his wife.

He wasn't the only friend we had lost. A Timorese staff member whom Brian and I had helped to get an overseas education, gifted with a talent like few others I had met then or since, died while taking a swim a few years ago. Osorio and I shared stories that lingered in our minds from all those years ago, the time punctuated by long pauses in which each of us was lost in our own memories of the two men.

Before long we came across a traffic jam. Heavy rains had fallen in the days before my arrival resulting in flash floods that were still working their way down the hillsides and gorges towards the sea. At one point the water was gushing across a road, chewing away at the tarmac leaving limited options for the trucks and cars piled up. With Osorio at the wheel we took the car off-road and across the flowing river, quickly leaving behind the minor distraction, but for the transport trucks hauling fresh produce to Indonesia and travellers making their way back to Dili their day was lost to the common curse of developing countries—poor engineering and insufficient funds to maintain the roads.

It wasn't long before we entered Liquiçá, the first major town west of Dili. For the Timorese the name is synonymous with a tragic massacre. Two hundred people were killed by rampaging militia while they sought refuge in a church during the months leading up to the referendum. Coincidentally, Osorio was there that April night in 1999 when it all happened. He had been riding a public bus heading back to Dili from Indonesia late in the evening.

'It was almost three in the morning and I saw the road full with blood, fresh blood.' His bus had come to a standstill at an Indonesian military checkpoint not far from the church.

A soldier boarded the bus, berating the driver, asking, 'How come you're out at this time? It's very dangerous. We are expecting Falantil [the resistance] to attack us.' Then, turning to the passengers he said, 'Look at the church, see what happened at the church.'

From his window seat Osorio could see bodies scattered in front of the church, some lying crumpled, awkwardly positioned as they had fallen, others lay more neatly having been moved from inside, all probably dead though he had no way of knowing. Two hundred people had been massacred that day. A subsequent UN investigation found that the Indonesian-backed militia, including some military personnel dressed in civilian clothes, had practised a peculiar initiation ceremony that saw them drink alcohol and animal blood mixed with drugs before going on their killing rampage.

Leaving the outskirts of Liquiçá, it was hard for me to appreciate the tranquillity without thinking of the past events that led to this country's independence. The civil war in the mid-seventies, a campaign of forced displacement and famine by Indonesia, an untold number of disappearances, the Dili massacre in 1991, and the violence of 1999 that saw one third of the population internally displaced, with another third living as refugees in West Timor. By the time I arrived in 2000 it was estimated that between 102,000 and 183,000 people had died through the Indonesian occupation as a result of human rights abuses from a population of less than 800,000. I could only imagine what it was like for the Timorese when each and every corner of this small country represents a tragic marker in their history.

As the sun began to set we reached the vast rice fields nestled in the low-lying areas of Atabae. From there it was only a short drive to the border town of Batugade and then we turned south-east, driving along the border inland until we reached Maliana where we would spend the night.

Our conversation over the long drive took us back to the nineties when we were both still at college. It was hard not to see Osorio as a much older man when we compared our youth. While I was carrying beer to parties, he carried arms to the resistance. As I play-brawled with friends, he was involved in a tit-for-tat of killings and retributions on campus. My focus was on writing a thesis, his on surreptitiously gathering covert information. Osorio was part of the clandestine movement; brought in at a young age he became a crucial cog in the effort to maintain pressure on the occupiers.

As he recalled some of his memories his voice rose and quickened as if excited by the recollection of the trials and tragedies. It's expected of people when telling tragic stories to do so in a sombre tone, to whisper in a remorseful voice. I took his enthusiasm not as a disregard for those who had lost their lives but as a sign of trust in me that I wouldn't judge him as he recalled what he had lived through.

While behind the wheel driving along the long coastal road, he shared with me the story of what had brought him to Liquiçá that night. He had been instructed to take one of only five satellite phones that the entire resistance had to West Timor for repairs. Taking them across the border went without a hitch. But on the way back it was just bad timing. The massacre had put the military and militia at high alert at every checkpoint. Instead of sleeping during the ride back to Dili he was taken off the bus, with gun, bow and arrow, or flashlight pointed at him as he was questioned. Although Osorio carried a West Timorese ID, the militia saw that he had an East Timorese name and his accent wasn't from the former Dutch half of the island. But at each stage his resourcefulness and quick thinking proved his saving grace and he managed to be ushered back onto the bus along with the others.

US Marines

As we talked night fell. We managed to reach Maliana late in the evening, meeting up with Filimino, a former staff member who had arranged a room for us in a local hotel. The next morning we planned to make the drive to Suco Lour, one of the more inaccessible places in East Timor—even with our 4x4 trucks we couldn't deliver shelter materials to the area. I chose to visit this village for my return visit as it had been one of the most in need then and presumably still would be now.

At around three thousand feet with only narrow dirt paths to drive along in 2000, we had to rely upon the US Marine Expeditionary Unit to lend their CH-46 helicopters known as Baby Chinooks to help us carry the twenty-eight tons of materials up the mountains. The Marines were due early in the morning and we needed to provide them with a cleared landing site. The agreed marker was our white Toyota HiLux easily visible from the air. My team and I enjoyed the sunrise from the mountain ridge along with some dry bread and fruit before waiting out the morning. The sound of the helicopter's twin rotors cut through the quiet morning air before we could see its colours against the crisp blue sky. For the first trip it didn't carry any materials; instead, as it landed in the clearing, a contingent of Marines jumped onto the ground and fanned out, creating a secure perimeter while we watched lounging lazily against the car. As the Marines positioned themselves into prone positions, guns at the ready, the villagers drew back, unsure of what was to follow. But as they watched me engage with the lieutenant they came forward, milling around us as we worked out the details. Once everyone was satisfied—the lieutenant with the drop zone, the villagers with the new visitors, and my team with the chances of success—we all relaxed and started to mingle. One Marine asked me what weapons I carried. Others engaged with the people trying to communicate and taking photos, some wanted to know about the history and culture of the people. I wondered what the villagers thought of it all.

This time round the journey to Suco Lour was more sedate. For a start, we made the trip during daylight. Along the route there were only friendly faces, whereas during the earlier trip militia were still roaming the border areas and we had been warned to regularly check-in through the HF radio in our car. Both times I made the trip on a Saturday, which is market day. On the earlier trip we passed donkeys laden with produce headed for the market; this time, having already sold the goods, their baskets were largely empty as they headed home.

Osorio and I arrived to Suco Lour at about one pm after a four-hour drive from Maliana. Along the way there were a few moments where I wasn't quite sure if the Mitsubishi Pajero would make it. Each time its underbelly screeched against a rock I thought to myself that maybe I should have rented a car with a higher clearance.

The village hadn't changed much from memory. It was still perched on a razor thin ridge-line running along the island's central mountain range. There was some construction activity, with a police post being built, but otherwise little had changed. Houses were perched along the hill side, the same tall palms still swayed in the winds, and just as before animals went about their daily duties in bamboo pens. We were unlucky that the village chief, Alvaro dos Santos, had left for Dili, and instead we were introduced to the head of the village council, Joaqim Ramos. Sporting what looked like an old-fashioned ammunition belt around his waist with a sarong and a long beard, he fit the image of a traditional warrior leader. After exchanging greetings we explained why we were visiting and in particular that we were interested in talking to anyone who had received the shelter materials that were distributed to the village ten years earlier.

He remembered the materials and commented that they were still used and in good condition. As we talked people milled around, dropping into the conversation as it suited them. There was no privacy in such matters. What was official business was everyone's business. I asked Joaqim about the helicopters and US Marines that helped us haul the materials to their village. I had long wondered what they thought of the military personnel, the huge helicopter and the expense of the endeavour when donkeys that carried goods to the market in Bobonaro could have carried the shelter material with far less effort.

'As recipients, we accept any support we receive.' It was a polite answer, a politician's answer. I didn't press further. Instead, I asked him what he thought of the foreigners who had come to help. 'I don't have a comment about that, but we thank you for that.' I began to think that either he didn't have much to say or he was being coy, worried about putting at risk any future help. Osorio's view was that Joaqim didn't really understand what we were trying to ask and he was struggling to explain it further so we moved on. We thanked the head of the village council for his time and asked if we could walk around the village, and he agreed.

When we first arrived a light mist was drifting through, though now it was slowly dissipating as we walked around. Like an unfolding storybook, with each passing moment the panoramic vista revealed a new layer: a valley, a towering mountain, a distant village. My eyes scanned the village for the familiar design of the shelters we had distributed. Spotting one, together with Osorio and a contingent of barefoot children in ragged clothes, a limping dog, and a coterie of people intrigued by the visit, we walked over to the home owner.

Wearing flip-flops, long pants, collared t-shirt and a cap, Adelio welcomed us to his porch where we sat pointing and poking at his house. The shelter kits comprised of sixty-three pieces of varying sizes of timber for the house's frame, forty roof sheets, four hundred kilograms of cement for the floor slab, sixteen kilograms of nails, and one set of tools shared between five houses. His was a standard design, square base with an A-frame roof. In a way, we were delivering prototype Ikea houses. We provided the tools and the materials; they had to gather the friends and neighbours to put them together. There were no instructions; instead we built one in each village, usually for the poorest or most vulnerable family—a widow or a disabled adult with children. From that prototype the rest of the recipients were expected to replicate the build, though some took liberty in redesigning them in small ways.

As the rains came we quickly learned that the wood that had been procured from Indonesia wasn't treated very well. It had a limited future in the wet, moist, and insect-filled climate of East Timor. So we went on a hunt to find a source of oil that could be painted over the wood to preserve it from the elements. What better place to go than to the military contingents and their vehicle maintenance units. They wanted to dispose of the sump oil; we wanted to put it to good use.

While others had started building new homes, Adelio had carefully maintained the basic frame, adding to it as the years passed. He used split bamboo for the walls and added extensions such as a covered porch made from corrugated iron and wooden branches. He was grateful for the shelter kits as I presume were the eighteen other families who had received support from us in Lour.

A group of over a dozen people had gathered around while we talked to Adelio, and it wasn't long before the inevitable question came from someone in the audience.

'Will new materials be provided to us? We need more help.'

I asked what they needed, making it clear that I wasn't with an international organisation anymore.

'A road!'

As the words were translated we all laughed, concurring. The second need was electricity. They didn't have any electricity—no intermittent grid, no solar or even a generator. Third, surprisingly, was water. Despite the heavy rains and lush landscape, they told me that during the dry season there was very little water. Lastly, they suggested health services. When someone fell sick they had to carry them to Bobonaro, an eighteen-kilometre walk that would take between three and four hours.

Had Osorio and I been adventure-seeking hikers passing through the village, we may have envied the inhabitants of this idyllic mountain locale with spectacular views and a warm sense of community. But scratch the surface and it's not hard to recognise the hardship. The list they provided wasn't extravagant. It comprised of what should be the most basic of services. I tried to imagine what it would have been like for them in the months after the devastation when in addition to lacking these amenities some wouldn't have even had any shelter. But responding to this long list of needs was beyond the remit of international aid organisations. This was no longer community development but rather the responsibility of the government to provide basic infrastructure.

There was little more that I could learn about our program so we started to thank everyone. As we were leaving, a young man approached us asking if we could take him down to Bobonaro. With room in the car I agreed; though one adult became five, with the addition of one child and two chickens. How could we say no? They all piled in and we left just as the rains started falling. It wasn't a downpour, but any rain meant what had been rough mountainous roads were now muddy rough mountainous roads and the drive became a test of not only the Mitsubishi's clearance but its handling and our off-road driving skills. Despite having a 4x4 it was a slow trek back to Bobonaro, which only made me wonder how they managed to transport sick or injured people through the rains along the muddy terrain without a vehicle.

Fish Farming in the Mountains

Earlier in the drive I had flashbacks to one of the more bizarre challenges we faced: coming up with ways to transport hundreds of live young fish from the coast to the mountains for a new fish farm. The idea built upon an industry that had existed during Indonesian times. Through the initiative of one of the United Nation's best sub-district representatives, Nicolas Garrigue, the industry was being revived in East Timor. Garrigue had worked with the community to write up a proposal that was then sent to us for funding and implementation. The idea was simple—dig holes, fill them with water, add fish, build a chicken coop above the pond, and watch the cycle of life work. A continuously flowing stream oxygenates the pond. The chickens' droppings help to grow algae, bacteria, and microfauna required by the fish. The fish are used by the owners to supplement their diets and earn an income that pays for the maintenance of the ponds. When I first heard the idea, I was taken by its simplicity. There was no need to create a new market, organise long-term training, or engage in extensive infrastructure development. It seemed a smart and sustainable solution.

I suggested to Osorio that we visit one of the fish farms we had supported. He seemed keen, so the next day we found ourselves talking to the head of a nearby hamlet in Suco Maliubu. In East Timor, the hamlet is the smallest administrative unit followed by a village, or 'suco' as it is called in Portuguese. Dressed in camouflage capris and a brown short-sleeved shirt with coffee patterns,

Silvestre welcomed us onto his porch. Clinging to him throughout our conversation was a young girl about four or five years old. Although barefoot and wearing an old well-worn t-shirt along with faded pink shorts, she seemed as happy as any child could be. Like so many other places along the inland mountain range, the limited amount of flat land made the environment a tight competition for space. Rice fields were pressed against a sports ground that backed onto a school that stood tall alongside a sprinkling of houses. Looking down from the mountain the view would have appeared a patchwork quilt with different shapes and colours stitched together. The chief's house was made with a concrete mortar finish that looked as though it was from before the last civil war. I wondered whether his house was the only one spared in the village and what that meant, or whether the whole area had escaped the wrath of the pro-Indonesia forces. I didn't ask as that was the past and I knew from my personal experiences with my relatives in the Balkans that people do things during times of war that they don't want to discuss when the fighting stops. And anyway, for all I knew, he could have successfully led the efforts to protect his area and that's why he became the head of the hamlet. It was neither here or there now, so I moved on to the matter at hand—fish farming in the mountains.

The deal we had cut with the community was that they would dig the ponds and build the coops while we would provide the fish and chickens. The fish farm at Maliubu was a single pond that had received one hundred and fifty fingerlings and fifteen chickens.

'Can you tell me, how did the community benefit from the fish farm?' I asked.

'We would share with everyone who contributed to build the fish farm.'

'How many people would benefit?'

'Not many as there weren't enough fish. The village chief would distribute them as they grew large enough, but this wasn't often,' he told us.

It wasn't a ringing endorsement. Despite the limited impact, Silvestre told us that it was the first fish farm program in the area. Being the first meant that other villages with communal ponds and even private owners stocked their fish from the one we had established. As far as he knew there were seven others in the area that had been seeded through this one. No one else, it seemed, had to overcome the challenge of bringing fingerlings from the coast to the mountains—a deceptively difficult task. To achieve the job we packed the fingerlings into large buckets with lids, strapped them tightly into the back of a four-wheel drive truck, and drove them very slowly along the winding dirt roads, topping up the water whenever necessary.

I asked the head of the hamlet whether he thought the contribution was useful.

'It was useful. The only problem was that we didn't have the experience to maintain the health of the chickens and fish.'

'But during Indonesian times you didn't have anyone with expertise in fish health either and you didn't face the same problems, how is that?' I pointed out to him.

Apparently, we had provided a particular type of fish, what he described as 'big gold fish', which were bigger than the previous type that they had experience with. It seemed strange that we'd do that rather than use the same fish that they had before. I asked how this had happened and was told that they had seen other fish farms with bigger fish than what they had in the past and so they thought that they would rather have the big fish. No one thought to enquire whether any additional support to the community would be required to facilitate this new variety.

'How long did the farms continue to operate?' I asked.

'In 2003 the dry season was bad and so the chickens died, the water buffalo came to drink the water, which destroyed the ponds, and as the water was drying out, we decided to give the fish away. Those who took the fish away still have ponds with fish.'

Could I count that as a success? Who could have anticipated a drought, and anyway, the investment lived on in other areas. Our project was the catalyst. I asked if we could see any of the working ponds, to which he replied that there was one within walking distance. So we set off through the rice fields then past the sports field until we came to the school.

The functioning pond was owned and managed by the school. It was a four-room school with 325 pupils along with seven teachers. I thought it would be quite a tight fit, but I was told that they managed to deal with the conundrum of too many students and not enough space by having staggered start times for the classes. Half the kids start early and finish early the others start late and finish late. In a country where teachers' salaries are low and infrastructure limited it made sense.

As we arrived we met a man who, while not associated with the school, was familiar with the pond. Seeing no chicken coop, I asked where it was, presuming that they too had been struck by the drought and lost their chickens. Apparently, the drought didn't kill their chickens because they didn't need any. The school's pond operated in a slightly different system. Rather than chickens, the food to feed the fish came from leftovers from the government's school feeding program. It was a clever way to utilise every resource without leaving any waste.

Despite the limited success, I was still convinced that fish farms were a good investment simply because they were what the community had done before we had arrived and they are what the community continued to do after we left. It's a simple but effective measure.

* * *

As the plane lifted off I looked down at the long white beaches, crystal clear waters, and small islands lying just off shore. It was an idyllic posting for a young aid worker. When Osorio and I first started working on the shelter program, we had a great time as we saw the length and breadth of the country. We would stop along the coastline and hail fisherman standing in their canoes and throwing their nets just off the beaches. With the fresh fish in hand we'd light a fire and cook a meal on the beach. Other days I would swim in the reefs off Los Palos or hike in the mountains. But there was another reason why it was a dream posting. The international community and the Timorese people were working together towards the same goal—rebuilding the country. It was different to working in Sudan prior to the 2005 peace deal. That conflict had been continuing for over twenty years. The people were divided. They had lost hope. A generation or two were lost to the war. In East Timor that small sliver of hope that had survived the Indonesian oppression through the efforts of people like Osorio had finally been given a chance to flourish. Independence was within reach and the entire population knew it. They were united in their efforts to make something of the opportunity. The sense of common purpose was palpable as we went about our work visiting the most remote villages of this small country. I felt privileged to be a part of it.

Ten years later and the country had changed in some ways while not in others. Villages such as Lour still didn't have access to the most basic amenities but a new generation of young Timorese were taking the helm in Dili. While the old guard was looking to the past, insisting on speaking Portuguese and distancing themselves from Indonesia, the younger generation were pushing the past aside. When freedom first came to the Timorese, it arrived with a caveat. The harsh oppression under Indonesian rule was lifted, but ownership of their fate remained out of their grasp. Some saw this as a good thing as they believed that the people weren't ready. While my dinner companions had taken this view to the extreme, others differed on more reasonable grounds such as what was required to make them ready. Would a long period of oversight and support be required or possibly a short intense stint that pulled the country onto its feet? The difference matters, but too often it's not even considered. Under Brian's leadership we had begun handing over responsibility from day one. He believed that what we were doing wasn't particularly difficult and a short intense period of training would suffice. The staff took his efforts one step further by petitioning headquarters to fire all of the expatriates other than Brian and myself. While I was smug with self-satisfaction then, in hindsight it should have rang alarm bells as a marker of the contempt in which many of the East Timorese held the foreigners.

During my visit back to East Timor, the value of Brian's approach of empowering his local staff was the single resounding message that I kept hearing from former staff. Whether it was from Filimino, the wise old hand who guided Brian as his de facto deputy, or Joey Ribero, a former commander in the resistance who despite being tortured by Indonesians distinguished the acts of a few from the good will of the many, the message was the same. They told me that without those opportunities to lead and manage they couldn't have flourished in their new careers and contributed as they had to government, business, or international aid organisations in more senior roles. The message was the same in Iraq, with people such as Nawal and those who had run IRO, as well as in South Sudan where Chief Aliyaza lauded Samaritan's Purse for having come with a plan to establish a hospital, did what they promised to do, trained locals to take over, and then left.

While handing over responsibility for running NGOs or hospitals can be done quickly, running a country is very different. Nevertheless, the United Nations opted for a two-year interim administration before handing over the reins. It was an ambitious time frame that required the right people; the problem was that in many cases they were the wrong people. The East Timorese I spoke to wanted expatriates who had a passion for the people they were representing. Instead, too many were bureaucrats fashioned to follow procedures, people who were more familiar with the culture of their organisation than the community in which they lived. Few understood their jobs as interim representatives of the people with obligations to the community as Nicolas Garrigue did; and yet that is what they needed to be.

I was content that our programs had served their purpose. They had provided emergency shelter to people whose homes had been destroyed. Admittedly, they were late in coming, as at least one wet season had passed for most recipients if not two before they received the kits. The fish farms seem to have served a purpose, though it's hard to say exactly how effective they were—it was the right idea, but with poor follow through. I was left in no doubt, though, that the best thing we left behind were the East Timorese we encouraged, supported, trained, and empowered. They are now scattered throughout the senior echelons of authority in this young country, contributing in ways that are long term and sustainable.

US Marines landing at Suco Lour

A house built from the emergency shelter distributions

Head of Suco Maliubu, Silvestre, speaking to Osorio and the author

Adelio's house in Suco Lour

PART FOUR

Reflections

It was something we had planned to do for some time. Having ridden horses along the same route as Lawrence of Arabia through the spectacular Wadi Rum, hiked through Petra, and visited all the Crusader castles in Jordan, we decided to drive to Syria. The drive was only a few hours from Amman to Damascus. The only logistical problem for most people was crossing the border. If you had an Israeli stamp in your passport then you couldn't enter the country. Problematically for me I was doing some consultancy work in the West Bank at the time and so travelling to Syria wasn't an option until I got a second Australian passport. People who knew I had two looked at me askance, but for those living and working across the Middle East two passports, even if from the same country, was a necessary accoutrement. Once I got mine and my wife had her UN laissez passer we were set to go.

In those days the drive was comfortable. We passed the wide-open spaces of northern Jordan before reaching the border where we waited for several hours until our passports were checked, and re-checked. We sat back and watched as officials shuffled paperwork, tapped at their keyboards and carried our passports back and forth. We watched as families were turned back for unknown reasons, as shifts changed and new faces came to the counter to look over the same passports. Then we were called up, cleared and on our way.

Our place for the night was a former Ottoman mansion, one of many that had been transformed into a boutique hotel. Walking along the cobblestone streets of the old town we passed stores selling carpets. We passed the Israeli flag that was painted on the street for people to walk over and spit on. We passed the Great Mosque of Damascus, one of the oldest in the world. Eventually we came to our address. From the outside, the old stone walls crowding onto the streets hid what lay behind. It could have been an accountant's office, a bakery or, as we hoped, a hotel. Once inside the purpose became apparent, as did the beauty. A passageway led to a tiled courtyard with a fountain and a few tables and chairs. Reaching up three floors on all four sides were the rooms. The reception was tucked away in the far corner of the courtyard. Plants flowed over the sides of balconies, giving the feel of an oasis within the city. Damascus had everything I wanted in one place: history, architecture, cuisine, and culture.

Our next step was Hama, a name synonymous with mass murder to another generation just as Srebrenica is to mine or Darfur to those a few years younger. In 1981 Bashar al-Assad's father, Hafiz, had murdered tens of thousands of Muslim Brotherhood supporters in response to an incipient uprising. When we arrived, there was no sign of that dark past. Instead of an Ottoman home we found a less salubrious hotel to spend the night before moving on. Had it not been for my penchant for street food we would have made it to Krak des Chevalier, one of the best preserved medieval castles in the world. It was a visit I was looking forward to, but I thought that it would simply have to wait for another weekend. It wasn't to be. The Arab Spring arrived and we never made it back.

Sitting at my computer writing these final pages I decided to check whether any of the Syrian boutique hotels were still offering rooms as the sixth year of the civil war ticked over. They still were. The prices hadn't changed either. This is one of the peculiarities of war. There's a dissonance between the stark images of shelled buildings, rubble piled across streets, and faces covered in ash that appear on the six o'clock news with the indefatigable reality of humanity's survival instincts. Life goes on. Young men and women still marry. Businesses still operate. Foreigners still visit. It's just a different cross-section of society that now has the money. In times of war it's the smugglers, militia leaders, gangsters, and military generals who can afford to live a notch above the others. It's their sons and daughters who lavishly celebrate their weddings in four-star hotels. Their businesses control the markets for the services others are dependent upon. The boutique hotels that I found on the internet offering one night stays at one hundred and fifty euros a night simply pivoted to a new client base. Just as they did then they will again when the peace comes. The warlords and their daughters will no longer be welcome, but instead a new clientele—World Bank consultants, visiting politicians, and Western celebrities—will grace their jasmine-scented courtyards.

Although the hotels haven't been booked, the aid community is abuzz. There is talk that once the peace comes, rebuilding Syria will be the largest reconstruction effort since the Second World War. Iraq was big, but it was never destroyed to the extent that Syria has been. The nearest comparison is Sarajevo. A bustling metropolis under siege for four years, shelled from the surrounding mountains daily. But Sarajevo was just one city of less than half a million people. At one stage, before millions fled into neighbouring countries and to Europe, Syria was a country of over twenty million people. For this reason, as well as its geopolitical importance, the country will not be short of attention from the aid industry. Donor funding meetings will be organised, commitments made, experts deployed, and thousands upon thousands of reports written. Iraq received US$60 billion in reconstruction funds between 2003 and 2013. The money was used to attempt the privatisation of state-owned enterprises, reconfigure gender roles, establish democracy, and teach the bureaucracy impartiality. Despite the extensive training, laws legislated and a replication of Western checks and balances, the reality was that corruption was still rife, politics had become sectarian, and Islamic State swept across the western plains of Ninewa, taking Mosul followed by a third of the country's territory. Something had gone very wrong. For those of us who were following the process closely it was apparent—recreating Iraq in 'our' image wasn't what the people of Iraq wanted. It was the same in East Timor, where international bureaucrats whose experience spanned every developing country and then some imposed a system that they were sure would work but forgot to engage the Timorese along the way. Doing so would have taken too long. It would have meant pushing back on political expectations in Western capitals. Will Syria be different?

The international community can approach the challenge as it has with South Sudan, Iraq, and East Timor by drawing up lists of things that Syria needs and then passing the hat around collecting a hundred million here, a billion there. With large sums of money, it becomes expedient, even attractive, for the industry to bunker down and manage programs delivering these 'things' in isolation of the people for the sake of their own security. The resulting bureaucratised development assistance meets transparency standards with every dollar accounted for on paper, but corrupts the development process. Aid industry experts will fly in and spread the good news of their 'best practice' approach. Their justification stands upon the flimsy foundation of the idea that rebuilding a country is like baking a cake: a fixed set of ingredients, regardless of geography, history or culture, spur development and stabilise states. Engagement with the people is unnecessary. Popular in this bag of tricks are projects that can be designed and sub-contracted without talking to a single Syrian; road building, refurbishing schools, and international study tours. But building a bridge, for example, isn't just about facilitating trade across a river, it's about building the capacity for that country to plan complex projects, integrating future maintenance costs into budgets, ensuring local businesses are supplying materials, and so forth.

The challenge in rebuilding Syria won't come in gathering the financial contributions required to pay for the effort, it won't be in finding the thousands of troops to maintain security, or even the logistics of bringing in the materials required to rebuild the country. The first challenge will be identifying Syrians who can contribute to rebuilding their society and play a part in the new one. Academics Paul Collier and Alex Betts found that although less than five per cent of Syrians came to Europe, the same group included between a third and a half of all Syrians with university-level education. Without them Syria will resemble South Sudan, where the people who remain are largely warlords or the poorest who were unable to leave. To prevent this Syria will need people like Iraq's Dr Safa al-Ameedi, who remained with the Teaching Hospital in the lead up to the war, stayed during the battles that raged through its wards, and continued to lead when the time came to clean up. He knew what was required after it was destroyed. Syria will need people like Osorio who earned the respect of his community through his years of struggle and then started all over to earn the respect of the international community with his expertise and ability, then drew on both to become a can-do man. Even bright young people like South Sudan's Paul, whose youthful exuberance will be needed just as much as his intelligence to forge a way forward. These are the people who will be needed to rebuild Syria, but they will be hard to find unless they choose to return from Europe.

Even harder will be the need to find the right international aid workers and experts to lead the rebuilding and set the tone for engagement with the people. Will the United Nations and NGOs find people willing to heed the words of Ayatollah Bashir, who told the parable of Imam Ali wearing summer clothes during winter and winter clothes during summer? If they don't, it won't be long before Syrian officials will be forced to send aid workers home as Peter from the South Sudan Relief and Rehabilitation Commission did, or local staff will be forced to petition agencies to fire their expatriates.

There will be a desire to send people who will tell Syrian women, just as women like Nawal were told how they should dress without realising the struggle that is being fought behind the scenes, to overcome millennia of religious and cultural norms and how their obnoxiousness may be undermining it. There will be those who will idly sit in the most expensive Damascus restaurants talking about the 'dirty' Syrians and why they don't need electricity. A flotilla of experts will arrive by road and plane eager to tell anyone willing to listen that their experience spanning forty countries can offer solutions to the Syrians' problems; all the while they will be housed in isolated compounds removed from the people. These are the people Syria can do without.

Alongside preparations to send aid specialists, collection boxes will be dusted off and passed around from one country to another at donor conferences. We will be told that the Syrian people need money. Reconstruction estimates put the figure at three to four times that spent on Iraq. But there is something more precious and desperately needed in a humanitarian crisis, and that is time. Had we more time in Lui, Chief Aliyaza Bilyali Dawood would not have questioned what we had achieved after a brief eighteen-month effort, as more time would have allowed us to leave something behind. He was right to expect us to train local tradesmen for the construction projects rather than bringing in outsiders, but time constraints didn't allow us that luxury. Susan would have been right had she expected us to continue to support her New Sudan Women's Federation in their fight against gender-based violence, just as others had helped make the Women's Development Group in Wau the success it had become. We failed in these instances and others, not because of a lack of money but an artificial constraint on time.

Governments have time. The Iraqi Department responsible for running the water treatment plants where I found Rasool working along the banks of the Euphrates may have taken a few more months than we had to start their work, but they had continued to maintain the units over the subsequent years. In hindsight, our hurried time frame seems unnecessarily contrived and counterproductive.

Time wisely allocated can mean the difference between a fleeting contribution to a calamity touching only a few and lasting sustainable change affecting generations. Syria or any other of the world's humanitarian crises need more time from donors to allow aid workers to do what needs to be done properly just as much as they need the money.

Finding the right people to carry out the aid efforts and giving them time to do what needs to be done may seem simple, yet it's eluded the aid industry in one humanitarian crisis after another.

* * *

As I'm making the finishing touches to this book I read that the United Nations has taken the rare step of declaring a famine in South Sudan. The country has gone from fighting oppression, to independence, and then to civil war in less than ten years. It must be a record, albeit an unenviable one. The figures are staggering—a million people face starvation, millions more have been displaced. I reach out to my friends but not all reply. I wonder whether they are casualties of the conflict or they just don't see the value of engaging with someone who came and went.

Scrolling through one article, I come across a picture of Bentiu camp, home to internally displaced South Sudanese. The picture has a setting sun in the background. The foreground is bisected by a dirt road separating the camp. I can see an ad hoc market for firewood and dried grass for kindling or roofing material. People walk along the road, their faces silhouetted. A boy carries a bundle of wood, a woman two jerry cans of water. Men huddle talking. In the middle ground, ramshackle tin huts covered in plastic sheets stretch to edges of the frame on both sides. The photo brings back more memories than the image conveys. I can smell the smoke from the charcoal burning in the cook stoves. It's a smell that accompanies the setting sun each evening. I can hear the birds screeching as they head home to the few bare branches that remain, the rest having been cut down for firewood. The chatter from the congested camp, surprisingly, isn't loud. I often wondered about this. How could so many people be so quiet? Staring into the photo I feel that I am there. The memory of walking through a similar camp not far from Bentiu flashes back. In that place, I remember children playing soccer with a worn ball that some NGO donated, a queue of women waiting to bend their backs against a water pump handle, and calls for me to join families as they boil grass for their evening meal. I have mixed feelings as these memories flash back. While they give me the chance to relive those experiences, on the other hand, there's a sad realisation that nothing much has changed.

On the same pages that announced the famine in South Sudan is an update on the siege of Mosul. Iraqi government forces are fighting Islamic State in their last stronghold outside of Syria. Since entering Iraq in 2014, the fundamentalist jihadist group has at various times taken control of up to one third of the country. The Iraqi forces are in the final weeks or possibly months of clearing the city, at which point the full extent of the horrors of living under their rule will slowly become known to the world. I suspect that no discovery, no matter how gruesome, will make the front pages as the brutality of Islamic State is old news. I had spent nearly a year and a half in the northern regions based out of the Kurdish capital of Erbil. My responsibilities would take me to Dohuk, a city just north of Mosul, following a route that took us through the same areas that were now being fought over. The scattered villages that I visited, with their clusters of homes lying off the main road, had seen war before, many times before. Sadly, though, this generation was facing the brunt of battle more often than its fair share. The grating sound of tank tracks against asphalt, the sharp rat-a-tat-tat snap of AK-47 fire, and the tell-tale shudder of windows distinguishing an explosion from a car crash would be second nature to them. Their senses would be attuned to the sounds, ready to drop to the ground or flee depending upon how their sub-conscious mind was wired.

It seems East Timor is not in the news. At least not on the front pages. I need to dig a little deeper to read about the Timorese. For the first time in their short history they organised an election without the support of the international community. It passed uneventfully, which sadly explains why it's not news. The two candidates represented the political divisions of old and new. Guterres was from the '1975 generation' in a race against Conceicao, who was the voice of the new generation. Despite the restlessness of the young rearing to take charge the sixty-three-year-old Francisco Guterres, a Portuguese-speaking former rebel, won the vote.

As I read through the articles, I grasp at my memories in a desperate effort to make the printed words real. I need them to bring the words and pictures to life, but often I fall short. My memories are fading as my life recalibrates to a new norm. Sometimes I choose to gloss over the headlines or even skip the articles mentioning the latest humanitarian disaster. Like a failing relationship that has tried one too many times to patch things over, a break is sometimes needed.

* * *

I'm not sure when it was, but not long after settling into a new life in Melbourne, I remember being struck by the paved roads, green parks, and functioning traffic lights. How strange, I thought—not only an infrastructure that functioned, but a society that was carefree. It seemed like a parody of life, a thin veneer that was just waiting to be peeled back to reveal a grittier reality. Despite being out of the aid world for a few years, my barometer was still calibrated for Najaf where the crackle of gunfire could be heard regularly. The mother who gave birth in the empty block next to where I was staying in Wau and then continued on her way was my yardstick. Life seemed so strange here in Melbourne. I didn't feel that I had come home. Home was there, not here.

Three years later as I'm putting the finishing touches to this book, my wife and I are living in a spacious home, two cars parked outside and a one-year-old baby wriggling her way out of a cuddle. Dijana gave birth in a private hospital with a midwife, obstetrician, and an anaesthetist in attendance. Anything less would have been strange. We changed. Our expectations changed. When Dijana was in Chad and I was in Sudan we were grateful for a few hours of uninterrupted electricity so that the refrigerator could cool a drink, or keep meat fresh that little while longer. When I look at our fridge now I feel a sense of frustration for having bought such a small one.

Privilege and poverty, like beauty, are in the eye of the beholder. Accepting the ramifications of this took me some time. When I first landed in East Timor all those years ago, the passion I had for the job was driven by a desire to see things built, children clothed, and people housed and healthy. After a decade of moving from one desperately poor country to another, the poverty became relative. Not in the sense of some abstract GDP figure, but relative to the expectations of the person standing next to me. Did they feel poor? What did poverty mean to them? It was a revelation that shouldn't have been a surprise. It didn't include anything that others hadn't written about before. Money aimed at helping the poor could only be well spent if how it was allocated was determined by the people receiving it, not foreign experts. But to do so requires years of engagement, patience, and partnership. The countless experts, policy makers and decision makers who make critical decision in allocating aid resources appear blissfully ignorant of this.

As a result, the aid industry's priorities don't always align with the people they are meant to be helping. For example, democracy is developed through generations of interaction between civil society and the state, requiring educated and independent minded individuals. Instead, in Iraq we followed a colour-by-numbers process. Step One: write a constitution. Step Two: establish an electoral commission. Step Three: vote. It didn't seem to matter to policy makers who wrote the constitution, whether the electoral commission could conceivably ever be independent, or that voting in a tribal and sectarian society simply amounted to a census of ethnicity or religion. Politicians determined that a vote was required.

Alongside votes being counted, the aid industry likes clearing canals, building schools, and conducting training. If we can count it then we can measure it. If we can measure it then we can make it serve us better. Or so the thinking goes. But for the Iraqis, their faith and culture are important. For the Timorese, it was respect. Dr Louis da Costa wanted the international community to remain longer, not to better entrench a system borrowed from elsewhere, but to provide advice for a future written and produced by the Timorese. In South Sudan, there was too much short-term thinking without long-term commitment. Oxfam's Abdulrahman Wandati succinctly conveyed this. Father Martin lived it.

Despite many of my projects not having lasting tangible benefits, much of the work we did was provide life-saving aid to desperate people in need. We were there when they needed us most. We were there to witness their plight. Not in a vicarious way that belittled their lives, but to send a message that the international community had not forgotten. Our presence didn't always fill every empty stomach but it did give people hope. But there's no measure for hope. Without a measure it doesn't get counted and if it's not counted it doesn't appear in any plans.

Dijana talks of going to Syria. A part of me misses the adrenalin that accompanies war and reconstruction, so I join with her in idle talk of packing our bags. It's an admission that I used to only whisper to others. Shameful as it may be to take pleasure in something so full of pain for others, I now freely admit it. Living the risks used to make every minute of every hour of every day come alive. My name was on a list of people to be taken alongside Fadi's, but for the grace of God or the luck of good timing it wasn't the both of us who were kidnapped. Seeing a child's cheek pierced randomly by a bullet shot in celebratory gunfire or leaving Raga days before an assault by government forces made me appreciate life in a way that I could never have before. But this reminder of the fickleness of life is fading just as my memories are.

Maybe it's time to be reminded.

It's not just about selflessly helping others. There's an element of selfishness—the opportunity to live another life, drinking palm wine in the mountain villages of East Timor, watching the elaborate wedding ceremony of a tribe in Darfur or sitting with the Bedouins of Iraq. For the briefest of moments, I am somebody else, a part of a culture and history spanning generations that belongs to others yet are being given to me to smell, to touch, to live. Their forefathers become mine as they share their ways of life, their language, their food, their pride, and their fears. They are fleeting moments leaving only the smallest sense of being them, nevertheless it's a privilege that few people experience and one that I long for once again. I wonder how the Kurds of Syria live their lives in the mountains of Rojava or what the beliefs and practices are of the secretive Alawites. I want to stand alongside them, hear their stories and, if asked, to contribute to their lives, their hopes, and aspirations for their future.

This time, though, I would do things differently. Reflecting on this journey and what I learned along the way, I realise that the aid industry needs to change as the world is changing. It needs to move away from contract management and the delivery of 'things' that can be counted onto an intermediary role, finding a voice that speaks across cultures connecting the interests of local communities with the wider world. Aid needs to harness both the ambitions of donors and the dreams of the people it is meant to assist. It will require a back-to-basics approach in which aid workers return to living with the people they are meant to be helping, advocating for those people and being of the people. We'll need individuals who don't mind sleeping in five-dollar-a-night huts alongside a menagerie of bugs, or riding in tuk-tuks in the summer heat rather than air-conditioned four-wheel drives. And importantly we need aid workers whose passion for the people they are helping gives them patience for change that can sustain them through the years of struggle needed to make any mission a success. They will need to be as familiar with the spaghetti logic of a makeshift camp as the international donor system. As the world becomes smaller and more interconnected, the future of the aid industry needs to be as go-betweens, positioning ourselves as people who bring the global to the local and the local to the global. Above all else we need to remind ourselves at every opportunity that the people, not the projects, are at the heart of responding to the emerging global humanitarian crisis.

About the Author

Denis Dragovic is an author of literary and scholarly works on humanitarian aid and rebuilding countries after war. For over a decade he was at the forefront of international aid efforts responding to major humanitarian crises in Darfur, South Sudan, East Timor, Indonesia and Iraq, where he led one of the world's largest aid programs. Seeing slave traders ply their trade, leading efforts to negotiate the release of a kidnapped aid worker, or helping to support the establishment of local community groups gives him a unique insight into the humanitarian challenges of the twenty-first century. Denis' on-the-ground experiences are backed by specialist knowledge as an expert on religion and rebuilding countries after wars. He is currently a Senior Fellow at the University of Melbourne and a Senior Member on the Migration and Refugee Division of the Administrative Appeals Tribunal.

www.denisdragovic.com

www.ingramcontent.com/pod-product-compliance
Lightning Source LLC
Chambersburg PA
CBHW021101080526
44587CB00010B/333